TEAM BUILDING ACTIVITIES for STEM GROUPS

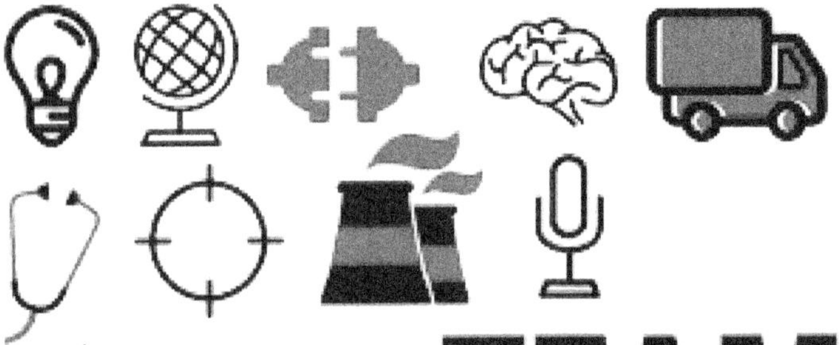
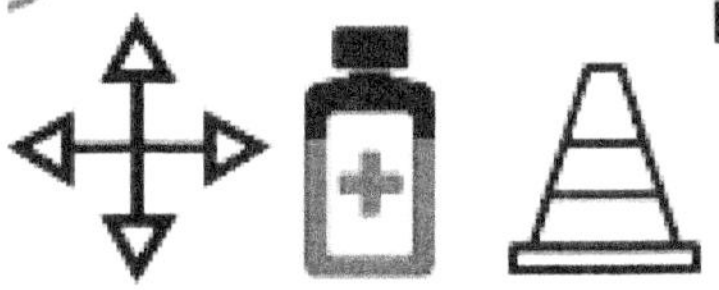

TEAM BUILDING ACTIVITIES for STEM GROUPS

KYLE PRICE & PARADIGM SHIFT

ISBN: 978-0-692-52682-8

Printed in the United States of America.

This book is dedicated to the many teachers, professors, organizations, and parents that encourage exploration, creativity, and critical thinking. You keep the lights on and the world turning.

Table of Contents

Table of Contents

Table of Contents

Understanding STEM-How To Engage Students

How many times have you heard that math is hard, no fun, or lame? As a calculus tutor, I hear those phrases almost every day, if not multiple times in the same study session. With students as young as elementary school and as experienced as doctorate level courses, there is a gigantic stigma attached to science, technology, engineering, and mathematics.

STEM (science, technology, engineering, and mathematics) problems and classes seem like torture to most students. We found ourselves asking the question that many people before us have been troubled with: How can we teach STEM concepts in a new way that engages and excites students at any age?

Combining my love for both STEM and team building activities, I started a search to find activities that really got people excited to learn new concepts and work together as a team.

The problem is that the internet is overcrowded with soft drink bottle rockets and vinegar volcanoes. While these can be fun and exciting in their own rights, these kinds of activities often neglect the teamwork aspect that is necessary for any design project, technological advance, or scientific research.

After these single-use projects are done, participants are often left wanting more only to return to math problems or science definitions. These experiments proved a vital point to us in our search.

Understanding STEM

Whether they know it or not, most students actually love STEM. If you disagree, just try to take away a cellphone.

Funding for STEM programs and careers is continually increasing in the technological age. Babies know how to use tablets and cellphones! The need for scientists, developers, engineers, and mathematicians is growing every year. Many teachers and organizations have seen this trend, but had a hard time getting students excited to make a difference in the world by pursuing STEM.

This book provides 50 fun and inexpensive activities that have proven themselves through the excitement, engagement, and teamwork building that we have seen at every event where we have used them. With each activity, you will see important STEM concepts such as the design process, understanding sequential logic, and comparing word problems to stories.

Questions for discussion are added to each activity to help participants gain an understanding of these concepts. Each activity is tailored for both fun and learning without sacrificing either.

We work with students across the globe. We have firsthand seen the impact that these activities make in students' lives. We have made it our goal to share this knowledge and experience with leaders. Whether you are a parent, teacher, professor, or organization, what you do matters. We want to help you inspire the next generation of scientists, inventors, designers, and mathematicians.

- Kyle Price

Team Building Basic Rules

Circle Up

The easiest way to introduce an activity from this book is to gather the participants into a circle. Circles allow all the participants to see each other and create a sense of equality within a group. No one stands before or above anyone else in a circle, not even the facilitator. Be sure to circle up the group as much as you can, whether it is in a classroom, gym, field or open room.

Break the Group Up

Some of these activities will work in large groups, but not all of them will. The best group size for the majority of these activities is between 15-20 people. If you find that you are in a group much larger than that, break the group up into smaller groups and have them rotate when sequencing into a new activity. This assures that the participants will not only interact with the people in their small group, but that they will have opportunities to meet other people as well!

Take Time to Make it Timed

Making the activity a timed event creates a completely new variation to any activity, and changes the dynamics of the group. Feel free to add this new element to any activity that does not already have timing as a variation.

Practice Makes Perfect

There is no better way to improve as a facilitator then through trial and error. Try out these activities with your family, your friends, and your closest group. Regardless of how well you know the group, you will discover new things about the participants.

Find the ones you love and try new variations and techniques. Introduce new stories and new variations that fit the personality of your group.

Remember: You can read about swimming, watch people swim, and learn from swimming masters, but you will not become a swimmer until you get in the pool. The same is true for these activities. Try them out, get used to leading a group, and these activities will truly open up your options as a facilitator.

Go Deeper

Many of these activities are often silly, fun and high energy, however they are also a great way to get participants to talk about themselves. Often we are too shy or guarded to delve into our personal lives, and these initiatives are an easy way to get our participants to open up and become more informal within a group. This will help groups to work more fluently and successfully in future situations that can become complicated or frustrating.

Team Building Constants

Many of the following activities differ greatly on energy level, age range and participant engagement. Regardless there are several "constants" with the activities that do not change regardless of initiative, location, or age. As a facilitator it is your responsibility to make sure these constants are followed by each participant and each different group.

Constant #1: Be positive!

Our good friend Mark Collard always says, "If it ain't fun, it ain't worth doing!" These activities should be fun and allow participants to open up to a group in a new and entertaining way.

It is important that all participants feel comfortable and welcome as they act silly, run around or share something personal. As the facilitator, you must always be positive and create an atmosphere that assures all participants that negativity, snickering or bullying is never an option.

Feel free to create these guidelines before you even get started, inviting the group to stay positive and encouraging throughout the entire day! Staying firm and positive as a facilitator will develop a sense of unity and togetherness that will allow all the participants to open up in their own personal way.

Constant #2: Be the example.

As the facilitator, you are going to ask your participants to do some crazy and wacky activities. You must always be willing to go first to show the group how crazy and wacky they can be!

Have fun, get into it, and show the participants that they can have fun too. Say your name in a funny accent, do a silly dance or create an imaginative motion for your name even if you know you will make a fool of yourself.

The participants will appreciate your initiative, your enthusiasm and your sense of humor and will more than likely be willing to do the same. Regardless of how the activity goes, everyone knows you are going to be participating with them and that you are having fun while doing it!

Constant #3: Be loud and clear.

Encourage each participant to speak up and share clearly and proudly. This teaches participants regardless of age or gender to be proud of who they are, and will create a sense of confidence within the group.

There is no reason to yell, but there is no reason to whisper either. Nothing will stop an activity in its tracks like a facilitator speaking so softly that no one can hear them! Stay positive and lead by example as a facilitator by speaking clearly and loudly to the group when you are explaining the rules and actions of the activities.

Constant #4: Be inclusive.

Whenever any group comes together, there can often be one or two people who would rather be eating dirt or tarring roofs than be with the group. It is important that everyone participates with every activity.

If you can get everyone involved early in the process while Breaking the Ice, chances are good that the entire group will stay engaged for the rest of the day's activities.

Be sure to creative an environment the beginning of the day where everyone wants to participate. Encourage the group to be inclusive to make sure everyone participates. It will be easier for you as a facilitator if the group's members are encouraging everyone to join in on the fun name games!

Constant #5: Be fun to have fun.

These activities are meant for the participants to have fun and interact within a group. Whether the initiative is high energy or low energy, it is important that group laughs, has fun and develops a sense of camaraderie.

As a facilitator make sure to gauge the group's "fun level" throughout the activities to make sure they are still engaged. Usually if a group is not engaged in the activity, they need to go back a few steps in the Pool Party Process. The activities in this book create new opportunities for a group to grow and allow participants to be creative, entertaining, and unique.

3-D Printer

Participants gain an understanding the basic process of 3D printing without having to buy an expensive machine.

STEM Field: Math
Number of Participants: 6-60
Time: 10-20 minutes
Activity Level: Low
Props: None

Set Up:

Group the participants together into teams of three people each. Have them either sit or stand in a single file line.

Objective:

After seeing a picture of an object, shape, or landmark, the person in the back of the line must have the person in front guess that picture correctly. Whichever team of 3 correctly guesses the object first wins the round.

Step by Step:

1. This is a no speaking activity.
2. Show the participant at the back of each line either a word or a picture of an object, shape, or landmark. Do not allow them to begin the activity yet.
3. After showing the object to the person in the back of each line, begin the race.
4. The person in the back of the line is only able to describe what the object is by drawing it on the person's back directly in front of them.

Step by Step

5. Since 3D printing is the focus of this activity, participants must draw a 3-dimensional picture. To do this, have the participants draw a 2 dimensional representation of the base of the object. After drawing the bottom layer, the participant should draw another 2 dimensional sketch of the object at a higher elevation. This continues until five to ten 2 dimensional sketches have been drawn. For a better understanding of this concept, search for videos of 3D printing online.
6. As the person at the back of the line draws on the second participant's back, the second person must draw the same sketches on the back of the person at the front of the line.
7. When the person at the front of a line figures out which object is being drawn on his or her back, they call it out aloud.
8. After a team has successfully found the correct object, they receive a point, and the person at the front of the line moves to the back. Everyone else moves forward making the person in the middle the new front.
9. Continue until everyone has had a chance to be in each position of the line.

Questions for Discussion:

- What made that activity difficult?
- Why did you have to draw 2-D sketches?
- How do you think 3-D printing works?

Facilitator Notes:

This game is a great time killer. You can just continue playing it until the group is ready to move on to the next activity. It is important for the integrity of the activity to keep the participants from starting until everyone has seen the design prompt.

Variations:

1. Another fun way to play this activity is to have the person at the back draw on the person in front of them while that person describes the drawing verbally to the person in front. This is a great way to add challenge while also speaking about the importance of design software in 3D printing. The software creates the design while the printer interprets the design as a model.

ABCDE

Participants gain an understanding of the basics of the engineering process.

STEM Field: Engineering
Number of Participants: 5-100
Time: 15-20 minutes
Activity Level: Low
Props: Optional paper and markers.

Set Up:

None

Objective:

Learn the ABCDE of decision making.

Step by Step:

1. Have the participants sit down near each other so they may discuss the next steps..
2. Give the group a fun scenario in which they are faced with a problem. This is generally best when they know a decent amount about the subject. (A fun setup is to tell the group that everyone is in a room with a tall ceiling and the objective is for someone in the group to touch the ceiling in this hypothetical room).
3. Let the group figure out how to touch the imaginary ceiling on their own without telling them any of the design process steps.
4. After the group has "touched the ceiling", give the group another scenario and problem. (Maybe they are on an airplane and the pilot has passed out!)

Step by Step:

5. This time, guide the group through the ABCDE of decision making:
   A. Ask questions to understand the problem/situation.
   B. Brainstorm possible solutions.
   C. Choose the best possible option to solve the problem.
   D. Do it.
   E. Evaluate if/how well it worked

Questions for Discussion:

- How was the first scenario similar to the second one?

- Why were you given the first scenario?

- How often do you use ABCDE of decision making? Is it daily?

Facilitator Notes:

This activity is designed to be an easy win for the participants and prove that everyone uses the ABCDE process on a regular basis whether consciously or subconsciously. Make it a little hard for the participants at first, but if the group comes up with a clever idea, reward it.

Variations:

This activity can easily be used to frame any other activity in this book, just guide the group through ABCDE as they plan the solution to that particular activity.

Add 'em Up

Different regions, schools, and even learning styles encourage different ways to solve problems and think critically. In this activity, participants are encouraged to think outside of the box and think critically.

STEM Field: Mathematics
Number of Participants: 20-100
Time: 5-20 minutes
Activity Level: Low
Pool Party: Swim
Props: None

Set Up:

Have the group form a circle.

Objective:

The group must figure out how many fingers are being held up by every one of its members as fast as possible.

Step by Step:

1. Have each participant hold both of their hands behind their backs.
2. On the count of three, have each participant hold up a number between 0 and 10 for the entire group to count.
3. The round ends when the group figures out the total number of fingers that are held up.
4. If a large amount (more than 1/3) of the group holds up the same number, the round must restart.
5. If any participant changes the number of fingers that are held up, the round must restart.

Add 'em Up

Step by Step:

6. After the first round, add the constraint that if the group uses the same method as the first round, 1 minute will be added to their time for the round.
7. Play the second round.
8. After the second round, let the group know that an extra minute will be added if either of the first two methods to count are used.
9. Play the third round.
10. For the final round, let the group choose whichever counting method they would like. There are no time penalties for using prior methods or ideas.
11. Play the final round.

Questions for Discussion:

- Which method worked best?

- Which method was most efficient? Fastest? Easiest to understand?

- Why were you discouraged from using the same ideas?

Facilitator Notes:

This activity can quickly cause debate or argument, while this can be healthy, it is sometimes best to lightly guide the group without adding strategy or suggestion. Allow the group to work through ideas, strategies, and debates unless intervention is needed. Trust in the participants' creativity and problem solving skills goes a long way.

Asteroids

This activity is a fun way to get participants talking about space and the asteroid belt.

STEM Field: Science
Number of Participants: 15-80
Time: 10-15 minutes
Activity Level: High
Props: Paper balls or stuffed animals (about 3/4 the number of participants you have)

Set Up:

Spread the "throwables" evenly around the activity area.

Objective:

Be the last person standing.

Step by Step:

1. Explain to the group that when you say go, it is everyone's goal to throw the throwables at other players while avoiding being hit by others.
2. If a participant is hit with a throwable, they must kneel down on the ground.
3. The last person standing wins the round.
4. For the next round, if a participant is hit, he or she must take a knee. This time, the participant may grab nearby throwables without moving his or her legs. They can hit other participants with these throwables.
5. For the final round, if a participant is hit, he or she must take a knee. This time, they may grab and throw throwables without moving their legs. If he or she hits another participant, they can get back up and resume playing the activity.

Bellringers

You never know how students are entering a classroom. They could be having a great day, or a terrible day. These are designed to get students focused, and have fun. They are great to build buy-in from your students.

STEM Field: Mathematics
Number of Participants: 1-150
Time: 5 minutes
Activity Level: Low
Props: Paper, Writing Utensils

Set Up:

None.

Objective:

Riddles and puzzles are a great way to start a class. The goal is to energize, and engage students.

Bellringers:

Palindrome Puzzles - A palindrome is a word, phrase, verse, or sentence that reads the same backward or forward

Q: What word becomes a palindrome when viewed upside down and backwards?
A: SWIMS

Q: Pronounced as one letter but written with three, only two different letters are used to make me. I'm crossed, I'm black, or blue, or gray.
I'm read from both ends and the same either way.
A: EYE

Q: What word, when written in capital letters, is the same forwards, backwards and upside down? It is sometimes high or after.
A: NOON

Q: What call for help, when written in capital letters, is the same forwards, backwards and upside down?
A: SOS

Q: How did Adam use a palindrome to introduce himself to Eve when they first met?
A: "Madam in Eden, I'm Adam"

Riddles

Q: How can you add eight 8's to get the number 1,000? (only use addition)
A: The key to this math riddle is realizing that the one place value must be zero.

$$888 + 88 + 8 + 8 + 8 = 1{,}000$$

Q: Two fathers and two sons sat down to eat eggs for breakfast. They ate exactly three eggs, each person had one egg. The riddle is for you to explain how.
A: One of the 'fathers' is also a grandfather. Therefore the other father is both a son and a father to the grandson. In other words, the one father is both a son and a father.

Q: Part I. What digit is the most frequent between the numbers 1 and 1,000 (inclusive)?
A: The most common digit is '1.' Can you figure out why?

Q: Part II. What digit is the least frequent between the numbers 1 and 1,000?
A: 0 is the least common digit even though 1,000 has three zero's !

Explanations: The digits 0 through 9 all follow the same pattern there is exactly 1 occurrence of each digit for every ten numbers.

For instance the digit 2 appears once between 10 and 19, at 12. And 2 appears once between, 30 and 39 at 32. However, each of the digits 1 through 9 also appear in other numbers in the tens and hundreds place.

Again, let's look at 2 which appears in 20,21,22, 23, etc.. as well as 200,201, 202,203..

So to figure out how to answer the first riddle you had to see what distinguishes the number 1? Only that we are including 1,000 which would be the first '1' in a new series of ten! In other words, the digit 1 only has a single extra occurrence (301 occurrences) compared to 2 or 3 or 9 which each have exactly 300 occurrences.

The reason that zero has the least (BY FAR at only 192 occurrences) is because zero does not have any equivalents to 22, 33, 44, 222, 3333 etc..

Q: A man in a restaurant asked a waiter for a juice glass, a dinner plate, water, a match, and a lemon wedge. The man poured enough water onto the plate to cover it.
"If you can get the water on the plate into this glass without touching or moving this plate, I will give you

$100," the man said. "You can use the match and lemon to do this."

A few minutes later, the waiter walked away with $100 in his pocket. How did the waiter get the water into the glass?

A: First, the waiter stuck the match into the lemon wedge, so that it would stand straight. Then he lit the match, and put it in the middle of the plate with the lemon. Then, he placed the glass upside-down over the match. As the flame used up the oxygen in the glass, it created a small vacuum, which sucked in the water through the space between the glass and the plate. Thus, the waiter got the water into the glass without touching or moving the plate.

Q: You have 8 dice, 1 is slightly heavier than the others but you cannot tell by seeing it or feeling it. You must use a scale, but the scale can only be used twice, then is broken forever. How do you tell which dice is heavier than the other 7?

A: On your first attempt weigh 3 dice on each side of the scale. If even, the heavier dice must be one of your remaining 2. Then you weigh the remaining 2 to determine which is heavier. If, when you weigh 3 on each side, one side is heavier, the heaviest must be one of those 3. You would then weigh 2 of those 3. If even, the heavier dice must be the one remaining. If not, it is the heavier of the 2 on the scale.

Follow Up Question: You have 9 dice, 1 is slightly heavier than the others but you cannot tell by seeing it or feeling it. You must use a scale, but the scale can only be used twice, then is broken forever. How do you tell which dice is heavier than the other 8?

A: The exact same way! On your first attempt weigh 3 dice on each side of the scale. If even, the heavier dice must be one of your remaining 3. Then you weigh 2 of the remaining 3 to determine which is heavier. If even, the heavier dice must be the one remaining. If not, it is the heavier of the 2 on the scale. If, when you weigh 3 on each side, one side is heavier, the heaviest must be one of those 3. You would then weigh 2 of those 3. If even, the heavier dice must be the one remaining. If not, it is the heavier of the 2 on the scale.

Q: Seven tennis balls are identical in every way, except that one of them weighs slightly less than the other six. How can you identify the lightweight ball with no more than two separate weighings using a balance scale?
A: Place three balls on each side of the balance scale. If the two sides balance out, you have found the lightest ball (the one set aside). If the two sides do not balance out, the lightest ball is clearly one of the three balls on the less weighted side. Now for your second weighing, place one each of your remaining three balls on either side of the scale. If the two side balance out, the lightest ball is the one set aside. If not, the lightest ball is obviously the one on the less weighted side.

Q: Three prime numbers add up to 100. Of the three numbers, one of them is more than a third but less than a half of another. Find the three numbers.
A: Since the three primes add up to 100, one of them must be even. The only even prime is 2. Therefore the other two primes must add up to 98. By trial and error, these can be determined to be 31 and 67. So the three primes are 2, 31, and 67.

Binomial Nomenclature

Biology can seem hard to learn, especially when you throw in a different language! This activity teaches some of the basic Latin names for use in biology.

STEM Field: Science
Number of Participants: 6-40
Time: 30-40 minutes
Activity Level: Low
Props: Markers and colorful paper.

Set Up:

On each piece of paper, write one word from the full Latin classification names (starting with kingdom and ending with species) of at least 3 well known organisms. We like to use human, cats and dogs. There should be a total of at least 18 pieces of paper. For example: on one paper, write Animalia. On the next paper write Chordata, etc. Next, split the group into 3 teams.

Objective:

Be the first team to complete the organism's name correctly.

Step By Step:

1. Give each team the 6 cards that correspond to the organism that they are assigned. Do not tell the teams which animal their cards describe.
2. Have the teams race to place the cards in the correct order. If the animal was human, the cards should read: Animalia, Chordata, Mammalia, Primate, Hominadae, Homo, Sapiens.

Step by Step:

3. When a team thinks they have the correct answer, they will get your attention, and you will check the answer.
4. If the group is incorrect, tell them how many cards are in the correct place.
5. A group gets a point when they complete the puzzle before the other groups.
6. For the second round, collect the cards and switch the organisms for each team.
7. After the second round, give each team the organism that they have not had yet.
8. The team with the most points at the end of round 3 is the winner!

Questions for Discussion:

- Why do organisms need multiple words to describe them?

- What are some ways that you tell the differences between organisms?

Facilitator Notes

For the integrity of the activity, make sure no one is able to use a phone or computer. Feel free to keep coming up with more organisms if you want the game to last longer.

Black Hole

Fill the Bucket is a collaborative team-building activity that requires participants to plan ahead to achieve a group goal.

STEM Field: Science
Number of Participants: 7-25
Time: 20-25 minutes
Activity Level: Moderate
Props: 3 Buckets, 30-40 throwables (yarn balls, Beanie Babies, etc.), a rope, and tape/rope/webbing to mark the boundary

Set Up:

Place the tape/rope/webbing in a straight line about 20' - 25' long. Place one bucket 5 feet from the line, another bucket 10 feet from the line, and the third bucket 15 feet from the line. The buckets need to be 5 feet apart, thus creating a staggered line of buckets. Place the rope in a circle with diameter of about 5' on one side of the buckets. Lay all of the throwables along the line on the opposite side of the buckets.

Objective:

To hit the team's goal by scoring as many points as possible during each round.

Scoring:

- 5 points for throwables tossed into the closest bucket
- 10 points for throwables tossed into the middle bucket
- 15 points for throwables tossed into the furthest bucket

Black Hole

Step By Step

1. This game is comprised of four (4) one-minute rounds. Each round has different rules, but before each round the group declares a group goal score. Also, before each round suggest (or require, depending upon the group) a two-minute planning period.
2. **Round 1:** Instruct the participants that their goal is to score as many points as possible by tossing the throwables into the buckets.
   A. **Rules:**
      1. The participants cannot cross the line.
      2. Once time is up, the participants cannot toss any more throwables
      3. The participants cannot retrieve any throwables from across the line.
      4. If the group throws all items before a minute, the round is over.
      5. Any throwables that land inside the rope circle are banished from the activity.
3. At the end of the round, encourage the group to help you add up the score. See if their score matches or exceeds their goal score. For every throwable that landed in the rope circle, increase the diameter of the circle by a few inches.
4. If the circle becomes so large that it touches a bucket, the bucket is no longer usable, and the black hole becomes even larger.
5. **Round 2:** Follow the rules for Round 1, but challenge the group to reevaluate their approach to the activity and see if they need to make any changes. Ask them to give you a new goal score.

Step By Step

6. When the minute is over, ask them if they set an appropriate goal.
7. **Round 3:** Follow the rules for Round 1, but this time give the team a new resource. Invite a participant to become a "runner," a teammate who can cross the line and retrieve throwables that have not landed in the bucket.
8. The runner can only retrieve one throwable at a time, and must hand the throwable across the line, not toss it. Encourage the team to pre-plan and then ask for a new group goal score.
9. If the runner steps into the rope circle or retrieves a throwable from the circle, they are sucked into the black hole and the team may no longer use a runner. If this happens, increase the diameter of the black hole by about 2 feet.
10. After the round, ask the group to evaluate their progress and determine the validity of their group goal score.
11. **Round 4:** Follow the rules for Round 3 (including the runners), but this time give the group another resource, "Backboards." A participant will serve as a backboard that will straddle a bucket, sitting on their knees with their back to the bucket.
12. Ask for a goal score, and complete the activity. After they are finished, process the activity with a creative and insightful debrief.

Questions for Discussion:

- What was one word to describe Round 1? What about Round 4?

Questions for Discussion:

- Did the group allocate adequate time for pre-planning the activity? What pre-planning steps did the group take?

- What ideas did the group find to be the most successful to complete the activity? Which participants developed the ideas?

- How did the new resources change your plan? What action steps did you take to implement the new resources?

- How did the group communication during the activity?

- Did any members of the group take charge? Who? How?

- Did the black hole hurt your scores?

- What does the black hole represent?

- How does a black hole work?

Facilitator Notes:

It helps to record the group's scores after each round on a white board or flip chart. This allows the team to see the progress over the rounds. Some groups need instruction on how to communicate during the planning period. Either provide that instruction or build up to that point throughout the day's activities.

Circuit Tag

This activity compares and contrasts two of the most important terms in technology: insulators and conductors.

STEM Field: Technology
Number of Participants: 5-30
Time: 10-20 minutes
Activity Level: High
Props: 2-3 rolls of painter's tape.

Set Up:

Lay the tape down in a large square in the activity area. It generally works best when the square is about 30'x30'. Next, create a grid inside the square by taping three lines of tape across inside of the length and width. The resulting shape should be a square grid composed of 16 smaller squares evenly spaced out inside.

Objective:

Don't get tagged by the "current!"

Step by Step:

1. Nominate one or two participants to be "it." From now on, those participants are known as the Current.
2. Explain that the current and participants may only move on top of the tape, the tape is the conductor. Anywhere else is called the insulator.
3. Participants may not jump or move over insulator.
4. Participants may only walk while in the circuit.
5. If a participant is tagged by the current, he or she becomes the new current.

Circuit Tag

Questions for Discussion:

- What is a conductor?

- What is an insulator?

- Why was the activity harder for the current at the end?

- Is it easier for current to move when there are a lot of people or just a few? Why?

Variation:

1. Another fun way to play the game is to allow each tagged participant to join the current. By the end, everyone will be running around as the current with only one participant left.

2. In this variation, when someone gets tagged, they must step off the circuit just within reach of the tape. They now become resistors. If a resistor touches one of the participants that is "It", the It has to slow down to half speed for a few seconds.

Coding Languages

Sometimes there is a big learning curve when learning a new programming language (Python, C++, Java, etc.). Sometimes there are only a few differences. This activity encourages participants to create their own coding languages to move a robot around the room.

STEM Field: Technology
Number of Participants: 10-72
Time: 15-25 minutes
Activity Level: Medium
Props: None

Set Up:

Group participants into teams of two.

Objective:

Create and adhere to a personalized coding language that is used to communicate between the controller (user) and the robot (system).

Step by Step:

1. After each participant has found a partner, give each group 2-3 minutes to come up with a programming language.
2. The 4 necessary commands that each programmer must use are: Go, Stop, Left Turn, Right Turn.
3. Each group must come up with verbal commands to tell the robot to do each of these functions. Bonus points are awarded if a group uses words other than those listed above.
4. Each group must also use at least 1 creative command. This is a command that both the user and the robot agree to.

5. An example might be the word "pineapple" as a command to do the robot dance.
6. After each group has come up with a programming language for their robots, give the users about 3-5 minutes to move their robots around the activity area.
7. Now have the robot switch places with the user. The new user may either keep the same code that was used in the previous round, or invent a new code.
8. After the new user has had a chance to move the robot around for about 3-5 minutes, the second round is over.
9. Now have each group split up and find new partners. Replay the activity and notice the differences in coding languages (the agreement used between each of the various teams) and the code (the commands specifically from the user to the robot).

Questions for Discussion:

- What were some different code words that you used?
- What was the funniest creative command that you did during this activity?
- What happened when your switched partners? Was this new coding language hard to learn at first?
- In what ways were the different coding languages similar?

Facilitator Notes:

It is important to emphasize the creativity of each group. This activity can become very boring if every group uses the exact same commands. This is why the creative command is implemented for each group.

It is ok if each group has a few things in common. This happens with actual programming languages too. Just remember that the activity is about comparing and contrasting the use of different coding languages.

Some groups need instruction on how to communicate during the planning period. Either provide that instruction or build up to that point throughout the day's activities.

Variations

1. A fun variation of this activity can be used to focus on teamwork, communication, and the general idea of communication disruption in coding. In this variation, have all of the users line up on one end of the room with their robots in front of them. Have each controller try to move their robots around the room without the controller moving their feet off the line. This can get tricky when everyone else is yelling commands to their own robots!

Constellation Matching

The public's fascination with space has only grown since the first man left the planet Earth. This activity is a fun way to familiarize participants with part of the great beyond.

STEM Field: Science
Number of Participants: 5-60
Time: 20-25 minutes
Activity Level: Moderate
Props: 12 Matching Constellation Cards terms – 24 cards total (see example below), 2 ropes or tape to make boundaries. You can download a printable PDF of the cards at www.myparadigmshift.org/stemdownloads.

Set Up:

Mix the matching cards up, and place them face down on the ground in a 6x4 grid. Place a 10-15' boundary about 15' from the card grid.

Objective:

To overturn all of the matching cards as quickly as possible.

Rules:

- Only one person can cross the boundary at a time to turn over the cards.
- You can only turn over two cards at a time.
- If the cards match, leave them turned face up. If the cards do not match, they are returned face-down in their original position on the grid.
- The activity is over when all cards have been matched and are turned face-up.

Constellation Matching

Step by Step:

1. Each Constellation picture should match up with the appropriate name for that constellation.

2. Encourage the participants to line up behind the boundary.

3. Following the rules, one participant at a time will come to the grid and turn over two cards. If the cards match, the participant will leave them face up and return behind the boundary. If the cards do not match, the participant will turn the cards back over and return behind the boundary.

Questions for Discussion:

- Why were the constellations named the way they were?

- What part of the activity best helped you remember the constellations?

- Why do you think constellations were important?

- How could the team communicate better?

Facilitator Notes:

Print your terms on dark colored paper so the words will not show through the cards when they are face down.

Constellation Matching

Facilitator Notes:

Laminate the cards for durability, the participants will step on, bend, and even rip the terms during the activity.

See the example of Constellation Cards below. Print off each set, cut them in half, laminate them, and they are ready to use!

Variations:

1. For large groups, create two or more grids separated by a boundary line. This activity is now a competition, however after the first team finishes the activity, the participants will help and encourage the other teams. Encourage both groups to individually rank their top four traits and present their rankings to the other groups.

2. Use any terms you desire to meet the objectives of your group. Replace the character terms with scientific terms, equations, Latin species names, etc. Literally any set of terms you would like for your team to discuss or learn.

Constellation Matching

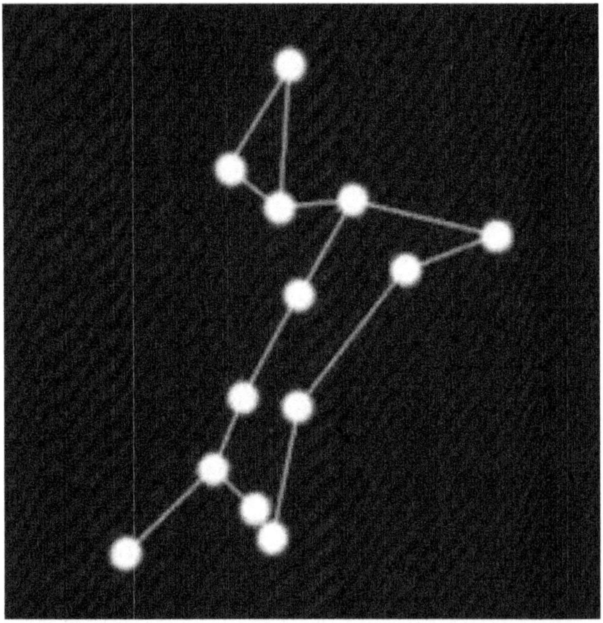

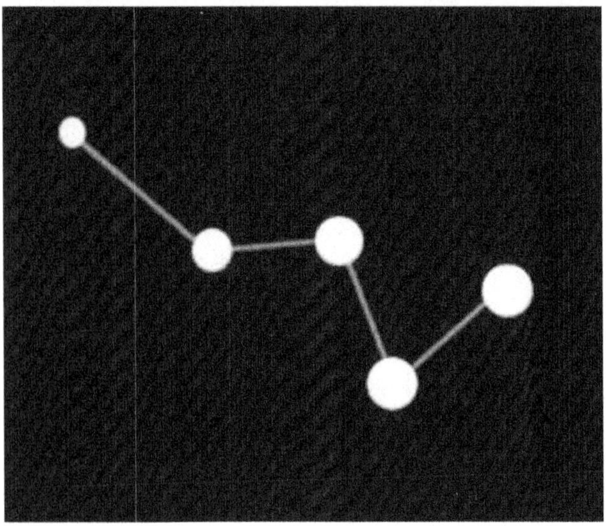

Count The Beans

Estimation can be a very important part of mathematics. This activity teaches estimation skills while maintaining the importance of working as a team to find a consensus.

STEM Field: Mathematics
Number of Participants: 10 or more
Time: 15-25 minutes
Activity Level: Low
Props: Jar of Beans, Paper, Writing Utensils

Set Up:

Count the beans in the jar and write it down somewhere that the participants can't see.

Objective:

To correctly guess the number of beans in the jar.

Step by Step:

1. Place a jar of pinto beans in the middle of the floor, and hand each participant a piece of paper and a writing utensil. Ask everyone to write their name at the top of their paper, and put Round 1, 2, 3, and 4 in the consequent rows.
2. For Round 1, the participants try guess how many beans are in the jar. Give enough time for each participant to put some deep thought into the process. It is important that each group member does this individually.
3. In Round 2, participants partner up and review guesses. The two then try to come up a group guess.

4. In Round 3, the two participants join another group of two and compare guesses. They then try to come up with a group guess.
5. In Round 4, the entire group discusses their guesses, and comes up with one large group guess. Eventually the facilitator reveals the answer and determines how close the group was to the actual answer.

Question for Discussion

- Does everyone agree on the final answer?

- How many of you think that the number you came up with is the actual number of beans in the jar?

- What are some different ways that you estimated the number of beans?

- How can the group come up with an answer that is closer?

- Who came up with the closest answer in the first round?

Facilitator Notes:

It is very important that the facilitator actually counts the number of beans in the jar for the integrity of the activity.

Each participant will use a different method to estimate the number of beans. Allow students to get near the jar, shake it, or pick it up, just make sure they don't open the jar.

Crazy Coordinates

Starting algebra can be a daunting task for a lot of students. This fun and competitive activity enforces one of the basic concepts every high school student uses: the Cartesian Coordinate Plane.

STEM Field: Mathematics
Number of Participants: 6-30
Time: 15-30 minutes
Activity Level: Moderate
Props: Tape, a bucket, a piece of paper, a stopwatch, about 10 throwables (wiffle balls, small stuffed animals, yarn balls, etc.)

Set Up:

Place the tape down on the floor making a 20'x20' square. Place tape across the square in both directions making a grid. There should be an odd number of tape lines inside the grid. This ensures that the coordinate plane has an origin. Place the piece of paper in the middle of the grid to mark the origin. Split the group into 2 equal teams.

Objective:

Score more points than the other team by placing the bucket at the correct location and throwing a throwable into it.

Step by Step:

1. Have the two teams play Rock, Paper, Scissors to see who goes first.
2. The first team will step to the bottom line of the coordinate plane while the other team watches.

Crazy Coordinates

Step By Step:

3. Each team gets 3 one minutes rounds to score as many points possible.
4. At the beginning of each round, tell the participants a coordinate and start the stopwatch.
5. One participant must take the bucket to that coordinate and set it on the grid. Another student will then attempt to toss a throwable into the bucket.
6. When a throwable lands in the bucket, a point is gained for that team. The runner will bring the bucket back to the group and help shoot.
7. If the bucket is on the incorrect coordinate, the team will receive no points.
8. As the runner brings the bucket back, tell the group another coordinate. A new runner from the group will take the bucket to the new coordinate.
9. After a runner rejoins the group, they may not be a runner again until the entire group has done so (to insure participation).
10. At the end of a minute, count up the points and empty the bucket. It is now time for the other team to go.
11. After 3 rounds for each team, add up the scores and declare a winner!

Some of our favorite coordinates to use:

0,0	5,0	-5,0
0,5	0,-5	3,4
-3,4	-4,3	4,3

Questions for Discussion:

- Did limiting the time make you answer faster? More accurate?
- In what ways did the team help the runners?
- Which coordinates were harder to hit?
- Which coordinates were confusing to find?

Facilitator Notes:

To make it easier on the facilitator, you may place numbers marking the x and y axes of the coordinate plane.

It might be helpful to write the scores for each round down so that you don't forget them.

Make sure the participants understand how the grid is set up and can use the coordinate plane before playing.

Variations:

Have the teams choose coordinates for each other. This involves a little more strategy and reinforces the coordinate system for both teams at the same time. This adds a lot more running!

Add different lines from which to score at the base of the coordinate plane. A shot made on the line is worth one point, 4' behind the line is worth 2 points, and 8' behind the line is worth 3 points

Desert Island

A simple way for participants to share their thoughts on technology and its use.

STEM Field: Technology
Number of Participants: 3-30
Time: 5-15 minutes
Activity Level: Low
Props: None

Objective:

Each participant shares with the group which piece of technology they would bring to a desert island.

Step by Step:

1. Give the participants the classic prompt "If you were on a desert island, and you only had 1 piece of technology with you, what would it be and why?"
2. Take turns sharing responses in the circle.

Facilitator Notes:

Usually students will say their phone or laptop. Sometimes, a student will realize that fire starters, knives, or mosquito nets are all technology as well. Try to keep from explicitly reminding the students of this fact unless it comes up naturally.

Variations:

Have participants share their answers as the shake hands and learn the names of other participants.

Equation Pit

This wonderful game is based off of the classic card game Pit. Equation Pit emulates the trading floor on the New York Stock Exchange, and is ridiculously fun and full of energy.

STEM Field: Mathematics
Number of Participants: 7-25
Time: 15-25 minutes
Activity Level: Moderate
Props: Equation Pit Cards - You can download a printable PDF of the Equation Pit cards at www.myparadigmshift.org/stemdownloads.

Set Up:

Print out Equation Pit cards or make your own.

Objective:

To "corner" the market and collect five cards that equal the same value (3-1 is the same as 2x1).

Step by Step:

1. Shuffle or mix the cards, and deal them to all of the participants.
2. Open the market by ringing the market bell, or just yelling market is open as loudly as possible.
3. Start trading cards.
   A. A participant can only trade cards by holding out one, two, three or four cards of the same number face down (2 cards that equal -9, for example). Encourage the participants to do the math in their head while playing.

Step by Step:

B. While holding out the cards, they will yell the number of cards they are trying to trade (2 if hey are wanting to trade 2 cards, not for cards that equal 2).

C. They will then trade cards with someone else who is trying to trade the same number of cards.

4. Once the player has collected all five of the same cards, they yell "Pit," and the game is stopped.
5. Collect cards, shuffle, and play again.

Questions for Discussion:

- How many different ways are there to get the right answer?
- What does PEMDAS stand for?
- What strategy did you use to win this activity?

Facilitator Notes:

This activity can be extremely quick and loads of fun. Sometimes a participant might win within a few minutes. If this happens, feel free to collect the cards, reshuffle, and play again.

This activity works particularly well for math groups or classes that are learning PEMDAS or just need a refresher. If this is the case, make sure to lightly review the concept right before the activity.

-121/11	-11x1
-45+34	(-6-16)/2
-10-1	-11:

Fast Fingers

Participants practice math skills by challenging each other in short rounds of addition competitions.

STEM Field: Mathematics
Number of Participants: 7-75
Time: 5-15 minutes
Activity Level: Medium
Props: None

Set Up:

Allow students to spread out in the activity area. Have them get into groups of 2.

Objective:

Add up the total number of fingers held up in the group.

Step by Step:

1. Once the participants are paired up, explain that on the count of three, each participant will raise a number of fingers (0-10).
2. Each pair will have a race to see who comes up with the correct number of fingers held up first.
3. After a pair has found a winner, the participants will move around the room to other participants and engage in another round of play.

Questions for Discussion:

- What were some strategies that you all used to figure the number of fingers?

- Were there any strategies that worked better than others?

Fast Fingers

Facilitator Notes:

This is a great chance for the facilitator to gauge a group's skills in STEM and mathematics near the beginning of a camp, class, or event.

If the students have more trouble with the math, make sure that you build your way up to the more intensive activities. This activity is also a great chance to examine different strategies and share the idea that different people think in different ways, and that is a good thing..

Variations:

- Another easy way to frame this activity is by trying to see who in the room is the best. This is known as Fast Finger Olympics.

- After each round, when a winner is decided, the loser becomes the winner's biggest fan. This goes until there are 2 massive groups vying for the title of Best Fast Finger Athlete.

Firing on All Synapses

The human nervous system can seem complex and confusing at first glance, but with this activity, participants take a look at how the brain sends messages throughout the body.

STEM Field: Science
Number of Participants: 12-120
Time: 10-20 minutes
Activity Level: Medium
Props: None

Set Up:

Group the participants into teams of four.

Objective:

Participants will move around the activity area while communicating with each other and observing the commands from the brain (facilitator).

Step by Step:

1. Have each group of 4 line up in a single file line.
2. Explain that each team has become a series of neurons in the human nervous system.
3. Since neurons relay messages from the brain, each team must follow the 3 commands that the facilitator uses:
   A. If the brain yells "twitch", the front neuron must move to the back of the line and the rest move forward one spot.
   B. If the brain yells "fire", the two middle neurons must swap places. The front and back neurons stay where they are.

Step by Step:

C. If the brain yells "reverse", the neurons must all turn 180 degrees around. The back neuron is now the front.

4. To move around the activity area, the last neuron of each line must give a signal to turn either left or right. This is done by tapping the respective left and right shoulders of the neuron in front of them.
5. To cascade the signal to the rest of the neurons, the signal given by the back neuron must be passed down the line. The front neuron will turn in the direction that they were tapped.
6. If a neuron network (a team) gets close to another neuron network, some accidental signal crossover may occur. Whichever neuron currently holds the signal in his or her own neural network may tap the shoulder of a neuron near them in another network. That neuron must then send the signal down the cascade toward his or her own front neuron.
7. After allowing the participants to move around and send signals for about 5 minutes, end the activity by yelling "Brain Freeze!"

Questions for Discussion:

- Why could only the back neuron control the chain?
- How fast do you think neurons send signals through the body?
- What kind of signals are sent through the body?
- How do neurons "talk" to other neurons?

Food Chain Evolution

Participants learn the "pecking order" of the food chain.

STEM Field: Science
Number of participants: 10-80
Time: 5-15 minutes
Activity Level: Medium
Props: None

Set up:

None

Objective:

Make it to the top of the food chain by beating other participants at rock-paper-scissors

Step by step:

1. At the very beginning of the activity explain that each participant is a plant. Since plants have roots, it is very hard for them to move. To show what a participant will look like as a plant, have them stand still and branch their arms out like a flower.
2. Each flower will have the opportunity to play another flower in a quick, single round game of Rock, Paper, Scissors. Have each flower find a partner to play against. To ensure a fair match, make sure that everyone uses the same rules. This generally means that the participants will show their symbols on "shoot" of the phrase "rock paper scissors shoot".To make the game more competitive, tell the participants that it will be a race amongst the groups.

Step By Step

3. Flowers may not move their feet at any point during the activity.
4. If a flower loses to another flower, they stay as a flower and find another opponent.
5. When one flower beats another, they move up the food chain by transforming into a giraffe. To symbolize a giraffe, have the participants crane their necks upward as if reaching for leaves from a tree. Players that become giraffes are now able to walk around to play against other players.
6. Giraffes are only able to play against other giraffes.
7. If a giraffe loses against another giraffe, they are then relegated back into a flower and must defeat another flower to regain giraffe status. For every level of the food chain, the winner moves up one level, while the loser moves down a level.
8. If a giraffe beats another giraffe, they become crocodiles by lifting one arm directly in the air and the other arm directly forward and "chomping" until he or she finds another opponent.
9. When crocodiles beat other crocodiles, they become humans by walking around with their hands on their hips as if they were superheroes.
10. When humans beat other humans, they take on the top level of the food chain by becoming T-Rexs and placing their arms close to the chest and making claws.

Questions for Discussion:

- What are some other examples of food chains?

Questions for Discussion:

- Where would you place humans in a modern day food chain?
- Which different kinds of food were present in this food chain?

Facilitator Notes:

Allowing "best 2/3" usually takes a long time. Try to avoid this if possible.

It is impossible for everyone to end up at the top of the food chain, but challenge the group with this to encourage competitive spirit.

You can stop the activity at any point, but allow for at least a few individuals to make it to the top of the food chain.

Variations:

1. Feel free to create your own food chain! You can even include the sun,, scavenger species, fungi, and bacteria.

Good Enough

In engineering, many estimates are made. There is always some amount of tolerance or estimation to an exact measurement. This short activity teaches that no one is perfect, and sometimes it is normal to have error.

STEM Field: Engineering
Number of Participants: 3-50
Time: 5-10 minutes
Activity Level: Low
Props: Markers, colorful paper, stopwatch

Set Up:

Give each participant a marker, paper, and room to sit down.

Objective:

Each participant must sit perfectly still and draw an exact circle in 60 seconds.

Step by Step:

1. Begin by starting the stopwatch.
2. If anyone moves any part of his or her body other than the drawing hand, remind the group to remain completely still.
3. After 60 seconds are over, tell everyone to stop.
4. Compare drawings to see if anyone drew the perfect circle (we all know how impossible that is!).

Questions for Discussion:

- Did anyone draw a perfect circle?

Questions for Discussion:

- Did anyone stay completely still for the entire 60 seconds?
- Did anyone accomplish the goal?
- Is the goal worth accomplishing?
- How did you feel about not being about to complete the task correctly?

Facilitator Notes:

Every single participant fails this activity every single time. By assuring the group that the goal was impossible, their spirits are not crushed.

Remind the group that sometimes, an estimate is normal! No one can be perfect. Educated estimates are used every single day in engineering as long as there is only a small amount of error.

Variations:

1. This activity can work particularly well after a challenging activity that frustrates the group. If the team was not able to complete the objective, or did so poorly, this is a great way to show that they can try hard and get better.

Greek Alphabet

Sometimes it can take a lot of effort to learn new symbols and words. This activity uses the Greek alphabet, which is used often in high school math and science, as a means to practice learning concepts and definitions.

STEM Field: Science
Number of Participants: 5-30
Time: 10-30 minutes
Activity Level: Low
Props: A marker, colorful paper, rope or tape (something with which to mark a line)

Set Up:

On the pieces of paper draw the symbol for each letter of the Greek alphabet. Underneath the symbol, write the phonetic word for the letter (pi, rho, epsilon, etc.). On the back of each letter's paper, create an equation that represents the letter's place in the Greek alphabet. For example, on the back of Beta, the 2nd letter of the Greek alphabet, you might write 17-15. Make sure to include mathematics that the participants know, but will also challenge them. Order the letters in a line in a random order. Place the rope or tape in a line in front of the letters.

Objective:

Find the correct order of the Greek Alphabet as a team as fast as possible.

Step by Step:

1. Assemble the group facing the letters behind the rope/tape line.

Step by Step:

2. One at a time, participants must cross the tape/rope line and move only one letter to a different place in the alphabet line. As the participant does this, he or she must share the name of that letter with the rest of the group aloud.
3. If two participants are across the line at the same time, or a participant moves more than one letter, add an extra minute to the group's overall time.
4. Time begins when the first participant crosses the line.
5. Once a participant has moved a letter and crossed back to the group, they may not have another turn until every other participant has taken his or her turn.
6. Time ends when the Greek alphabet has been placed in the correct order.

Questions for Discussion:

- What was the hardest part of that activity?

- Which letters were harder to pronounce than others?

- On a scale of 0-5, how anxious do you usually feel when you have to learn a new word or symbol in science and math?

Facilitator Notes:

Don't tell the participants about the equations on the back, this is part of them figuring out the answer. It seems impossible and hard at first, but eventually using the symbols becomes easier and easier.

Gridwalker

One of the most important lessons for an engineer is that of the iterative process of design and reverse engineering. In this activity, participants must use sequential reasoning to figure out the code and find a way through the grid.

STEM Field: Engineering
Number of Participants: 5-25
Time: 15-30 minutes
Activity Level: Low-Moderate
Props: Gridwalk Tarp and Gridwalk Map

Setup:

Get a tarp (preferably), a sheet, or just some tape on the ground and make a 7x7 grid of squares with each square being 1 square foot.

Objective:

For the entire group to cross the grid following the pre-determined path.

Step by Step:

1. One participant on the grid at a time.
2. If the participant steps on the wrong squares (not in the direction of the path), the entire group must start over.
3. After stepping on a wrong square, the participant must leave the grid in the exact order in which they entered the grid (basically walking the path backwards).
4. If a person does not follow the path correctly, they lose their verbal communication for the rest of the activity.

Step by Step:

5. After a participant crosses the entire path on the grid and gets to the other side, they lose verbal and nonverbal communication abilities. We do this so that those students who do not pay any attention must pay the consequences.

Questions for Discussion:

- Did you ever step on the wrong square multiple times?

- Are their ever times in your life you feel like you are messing up all of the time?

- How have you learned from your mistakes and changed you behavior?

Facilitator Notes:

When I am designing the Gridwalk path (see below), I try to make sure the participants do not have to repeat steps or go backwards. I like to emphasize the fact that you want to fail forward by moving in a positive direction.

Gridwalk Map

(Feel free to make your own path)

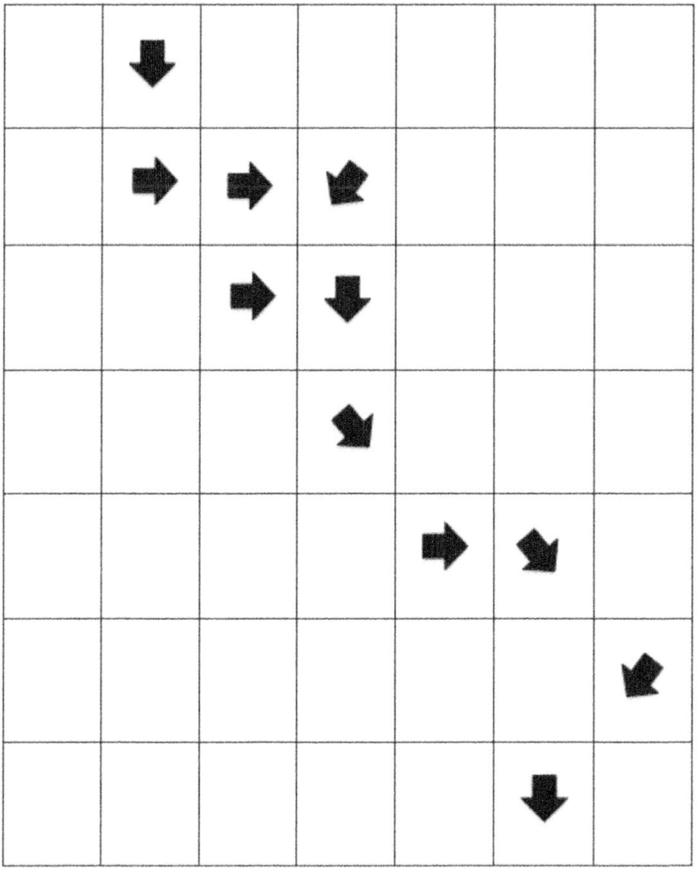

How Much?

Participants try to estimate some basic SI measurements used in STEM.

STEM Field: Engineering
Number of Participants: 3-50
Time: 10-15 minutes
Activity Level: Low
Props: A stopwatch, a tape measure/yard stick, pieces of paper, markers, a roll of tape

Set Up:

Place a line of tape on the ground about 10 feet long. Give each participant a piece of paper and a marker.

Objective:

See which participant can get the closest to the SI base units of time and length (seconds and meters).

Step by Step:

1. For the first round, have the participants close their eyes.
2. Start the stopwatch.
3. Instruct the participants to open their eyes when they think 1 minute has passed. The closest participant to the correct time is the winner.
4. For the second round, have each participant write his or her name on their piece of paper.
5. Have each participant place his or her paper where he or she thinks 1 foot is, starting at the beginning of the tape line.
6. Have the participants guess how far a yard is.

How Much?

Step by Step:

7. Have the participants guess how far a meter is.
8. As with the first round, the closest person to each correct measurement is the winner!

Questions for Discussion:

- Which was harder, the first round, or the second? Why?

- Did you travel further than you anticipated during the activity?

- Did you do better after watching others complete the activity?

Facilitator Notes:

If you want to come up with a crazy unit of length, have fun with it. It is fun to ask participants how far they think a fathom is without telling them that it is just 6 feet long.

Variations:

1. Depending on your space try a much longer length. See if it changes how well the participants perform.

Human Machines

Participants take a look at some classic machines throughout time..

STEM Field: Technology
Number of Participants: 9-60
Time: 10-20 minutes
Activity Level: Medium
Props: None

Set Up:

Break the participants up into groups of three or four.

Objective:

Bring back some nostalgia by having each group of participants become different technologies across time by using only their bodies.

Step by Step:

1. After breaking the group into teams, explain that there will be a contest to see which team has the best representation of the technology that you call out.
2. Bonus points go to whichever teams come up with great designs in a short amount of time.
3. After each team becomes the technology, go around the room and point out the interesting and fun designs.
4. There can be as many of as few rounds as you'd like! Just make sure the teams are still engaged and energized to play.

Step by Step:

5. Some of our favorite technologies to call out during this activity:
   1. Wheel
   2. CD Player
   3. Rotary Phone
   4. Cell Phone
   5. Dish Washer
   6. Dryer
   7. Refrigerator
   8. Sink
   9. Computer
   10. Television
   11. Jet Pack

Questions for Discussion:

- How many different designs were there for _____? (Television, for example)

- Which groups achieved the goal of creating the technology that I called out?

- What were some ways that you came up with different designs for the same technology?

- By show of hands, how many of you would describe the wheel as technology?

Facilitator Notes:

Every team wants to feel valued in this activity. Make sure to find something positive about each design throughout the activity. Be generous with praise while remaining honest.

Human Mastermind

Permutations and combinations are an important concept to grasp in the field of mathematics and statistics. This activity is an example of a permutation, since the order of participants matters.

STEM Field: Mathematics
Number of Participants: 10-20
Time: 10-15 minutes
Activity Level: Low
Props: Paper, Writing Utensils

Set Up:

Place four pieces of paper on the floor, and write 1, 2, 3, or 4 on the pages.

Objective:

To correctly place people on their number.

Step by Step:

1. Before the group starts the activity, pick a person to stand on each piece of paper (do not share this with the group). Write this down to help you facilitate the activity.
2. Once the group is ready, tell them that each of them serves a purpose in their quest to achieve this activity. You have selected four people who have the opportunity to represent the group on the different pieces of paper.
3. Ask the group to place one person on each piece of paper, and you will tell them two different things:
   A. How many of them should be on the pages.
   B. How many of them are in the correct position.

Step by Step:

4. The group has to get the exact person on each page that you picked earlier. Each time they put four people on the pages, you tell them the two things. Continue until they get it correct.

Questions for Discussion:

- What is the difference between permutation and combination?

- When did you finally realize the correct people to put on the numbers?

- How did the people that weren't on the numbers stay engaged?

Facilitator Notes:

It is easy for participants that aren't directly involved in this activity to lose interest and disengage. To keep this from happening, encourage them to cheer on their team and help solve the problem of who is in the correct spot.

Engineers must work together to be productive. Constraints can yield way to creativity. This activity merges these two ideas in a race against time to build the tallest tower.

STEM Field: Engineering
Number of Participants: 10-40
Time: 15-20 minutes
Activity Level: Low
Pool Party: Swim
Props: 30 straws per team, stopwatch

Set Up:

Break the group up evenly into two or three teams. You might supply each team with a desk or table to use as a base for building, but this is not necessary. Give each team 30 straws.

Objective:

Build the tallest tower made of only straws within 10 minutes.

Step by Step:

1. When each team has received their straws,begin the activity by starting the timer.
2. After about 5 minutes of building on their towers, stop the participants and the timer to explain that sometimes engineers face constraints while building. This can be a budget, lack of materials, etc. to simulate this, the participants may only work on the tower with one hand for the rest of the activity. Resume the timer.

Step by Step:

3. When three minutes are left on the activity, stop the timer to tell the participants that sometimes engineers must work together on a global scale. The team has been outsourced to Burkina Faso (any exotic country of your choosing) and may no longer speak for the remainder of the activity.
4. When the time is up, compare tower heights and declare a winner.

Questions for Discussion:

- What are some constraints that engineers might face while working on a project?
- Did the design of the tower change when you found out that you could only use one hand each?
- Did not being able to speak keep you from finishing the tower?
- Did anyone use the original design for the tower that you had planned?

Facilitator Notes:

Feel free to give the teams a few minutes to plan before working on the towers and touching the supplies. Disallow any outside supplies including scissors. This is a way for the participants to think creatively.

Variations:

1. Instead of outsourcing the company and disallowing verbal communication, you could have one person from each team decide to work for another company. Have them each change to a different team.

I'm a Starfish

Students learn about the field of biomimetics by mimicking the behavior and characteristics of animals.

STEM Field: Engineering
Number of Participants: 10-80
Time: 5-15 minutes
Activity Level: High
Props: None

Set Up:

Have the group spread out in the activity area.

Objective:

Become an assortment of animals based on prompting by the facilitator.

Step by Step:

1. Explain to the group that there is a branch of engineering and design known as biomimetics/biomimicry. This means that engineers observe characteristics of living organisms and adapt those characteristics into products to be used by humans (an example is how Velcro was developed by noticing the hooks on burs).
2. Each participant will now see how the "biomimetics modeling process" works. This of course is nothing more than a fun and imaginary way to frame the activity.Start trading cards.
3. Tell the participants that the rules are simple, "Say as I say; do as I do."

I'm a Starfish

Step by Step:

4. Begin the activity by jumping up in the air and spreading your arms and legs out and yelling "I'm a starfish" repeatedly. Soon, there will be an entire room filled with starfish jumping and spreading their limbs.
5. After the first round, create more animal name and motion combinations. A few of our favorite are:
   A. I'm an elephant (wave one arm as a trunk from your face).
   B. I'm a monkey (wave your hands around and act like a monkey).
   C. I'm a fish (make a fish face).
   D. I'm a T-Rex (hold your arms closer to your chest and bite the air).

Facilitator Notes:

This activity generally requires a little bit of time for the participants to know each other and feel comfortable with acting silly around each other. It is a great way to open up the second day of a camp or end the first day with energy.

If Then Else

A major push in modern STEM curriculum focuses on the importance of coding and computer science. It's said that the earlier someone starts, the better. This activity is a fun way to introduce beginner concepts of coding.

STEM Field: Engineering
Number of Participants: 10-70
Time: 10-15 minutes
Activity Level: Medium
Props: None

Set Up:

Have the participants spread out in the activity area and face you.

Objective:

Follow the code as closely as possible to win!

Step by Step:

1. Begin the activity by explaining "if-then" statements. These are conditional statements that take an input (if X happens) and apply some sort of action based on the input (then Y happens). For example, if "I raise my right hand, then you raise your right hand". When I raise my right hand (the input) everyone else should raise their right hands (the response). When I raise my left hand, no one should raise their hands.

If Then Else

Step by Step:

2. A few tried and true "if-then" statements for Round 1 are:
    A. If I raise my right hand, then you raise your left hand.
    B. If I raise my left hand, then you raise your left hand.
    C. If I wave, you touch your nose.
    D. If I say Hillshire, you say Farms, Hillshire Farms, Go Meat!.
3. Another phrase can be added to the "if-then" statement to add an additional response if the input is not seen. This is called an "if-the-else" statement. For example, "If I raise my right hand, then you raise your right hand, else you raise your left foot." When you raise your right hand, the group should all raise their right hands. If you do any other action besides raising your right hand, they should lift their left feet.
4. Some of our favorite "if-then-else" statements are:
    1. If I jump left, then you jump left, else you jump right.
    2. If I jump left, then you jump right, else you jump left.
    3. If I put my right hand in, then you put your right hand in, else you "shake it all about."

Questions for Discussion:

- What is an example of an "if-then" statement?

- What does "input" mean? "Response"?

Invent Anything

Participants take 5-10 minutes to unleash their creativity and brainstorm the coolest possible invention that could ever be made.

STEM Field: Technology
Number of Participants: 3-75
Time: 10-15 minutes
Activity Level: Low
Props: Colorful Paper, Markers

Set Up:

Place the markers and paper around the room so the participants can easily grab something to write with and something to write on.

Objective:

To see who can invent the coolest/most interesting/funniest invention ever in a judgement free zone.

Step by Step:

1. Explain to the participants that some of the greatest inventions of all time seemed a little crazy to begin with. Can you imagine a machine that lets a person fly? That's crazy!
2. Challenge the participants to draw or write out an invention that can make the world a better place. Bonus points for originality and creativity!
3. The students can either take turns to share their inventions or the facilitator can take a few samples from the crowd. This is a great chance for the more reserved participants to actively engage with the group. Everyone wants to be valued!

Questions for Discussion:

- What was the most interesting invention in your opinion?
- What inventions have already been created that are similar to your proposed invention?
- What would be the next steps to make your invention become a reality?
- What inventions do you think would seem crazy when they were introduced?

Facilitator Notes:

One of the best parts of this activity is that it encourages an anti-judgement zone. This helps create a group social contract to show that the group should value and respect each other.

This activity is helpful in engaging the more artistic stunts in the group. Feel free to be generous with generous praise.

Variations:

1. If you are running short on time, you can always have the participants take a minute or two to come up with an invention, and then mingle and share their invention with others.

Longest Bridge

Participants gain an understanding of design constraints and structural engineering by building a bridge made only of paper.

STEM Field: Engineering
Number of Participants: 8-60
Time: 30-60 minutes
Activity Level: Low
Props: Two chairs per team and 25 sheets of construction paper per team.

Set Up:

For each team, place the two chairs about 12 or 13 feet apart with the seats either facing each other or away from each other. Place 25 sheets of construction paper in one of the chairs.

Objective:

Using only construction paper, create a bridge between the chairs that is longer than any other team's bridge.

Step by Step:

1. Once the objective is explained, give each team a 5 minute planning period. During this time, they are not allowed to start working on the bridge.
2. After the planning period, give an extra 5 minutes for "machining" the necessary pieces. Participants are allowed to tear or fold the paper, but remind them that they only have 25 pieces of paper. There are no replacements.
3. After the planning and machining rounds, the activity begins. Give the participants X minutes to build their bridges.

Step by Step:

4. After the bridges are complete, compare the lengths and declare a winner!

Questions for Discussion:

- What made this activity hard?
- What was easy about this activity?
- On a scale of 1-5, how did the planning period help your team?
- What were your initial thoughts about this activity? (Usually they think it is impossible)

Facilitator Notes:

It is very important that the groups use only construction paper to support the bridges. This means that each bridge should stand alone between the two chairs while being judged.

It is difficult to keep everyone engaged in this activity if there are more than 10-15 participants per group. In this case, encourage the other participants to include those that get bored, tired, or shy.

Let at least 1 bridge be completed before ending the activity, even if the time has run out.

Mad Lib

Word problems are often difficult for students to grasp. The connection between the story and mathematic formulas is often lost. This activity is designed to help students connect the idea of story to math, and see how word problems are real world applications of mathematic principles.

STEM Field: Mathematics
Number of Participants: 1-100
Time: 10-60 minutes
Activity Level: Low
Props: Paper and writing utensils

Set Up:

Each student should have a piece of paper and writing utensil to answer questions and create. This can also be used as a group exercise.

Objective:

Have students create a story. Then implement mathematic elements into the story.

Step By Step:

1. Either print this story for each student to complete, or read aloud asking for answers from the group. Note: If space allows, having students act out this fun story is a blast!
2. You can recreate the stories below or download a printable PDF at www.myparadigmshift.org/stemdownloads.

Mad Lib

One sunny day, __________ (*student name*) and ____________ (*student name*) were planning a fundraiser. They were amazed when they saw________ (*student name*) and ____________ (*student name*) playing keep-away with ____________ (*student name*) on the playground. He/She kept shouting "no fair guys!" This alerted ____________ (*student name*) who was walking his/her dog, ____________ (*student name*). The two walked towards them but were stopped by three robots ____________ (*student name*), ____________ (*student name*) and __________ (*student name*). ____________ (*student name*) heard all this and came walking up like a monkey. It was all very troubling. ____________ (*student name*) and ____________ (*student name*) started to cry very loudly. ____________ (*student name*) and ____________ (*student name*), the police officers, were driving by in their squad car, so they turned their sirens on. As soon as they pulled up, the keep-away game ended, and all left the went back to class!

Read (and act out) this slightly different story with mathematic elements.

One sunny day, __________ (*student name*) and ____________ (*student name*) were planning a fundraiser. They wanted to raise $ ____________ (*dollar amount*) They were amazed when they saw ____________ (*student name*) and ____________ (*student name*) playing a game with robots ____________ (*student name*), and ____________ (*student name*) on the playground. They realized they could charge people to play with the robots as a fundraiser. (cont. below)

Mad Lib

Robot 1, ____________ (*student name*), was a fast robot and more fun. They could charge $ ______________ (*dollar amount*) per turn for this robot. Robot 2, ____________ (*student name*), was a slow robot, and they could only charge $ ______________ (*dollar amount*) per turn. Since robots are expensive, only ________ (*number*) robots could be used. How many turns with each robot would they have to sell to reach their goal?

Have students create their own story including the following elements:

1. Main characters
   - Example: Students planning a fundraiser
2. Characters Objective
   - Example: Raise $ ___________
3. Rate 1
   - Example: Fast Robot $____/Turn
4. Rate 2
   - Example: Slow Robot $____/Turn
5. Number
   - Example: Only ________ (number) robots could be used.

Questions for Discussion:

- How many turns with each robot must they sell?

Facilitator Notes:

The real power of this exercise is to focus on the story and creation of story. This will help students see how mathematic elements are displayed in real world examples.

Magic Swinging Door

This challenging activity encourages participants to think outside of the box.

STEM Field: Mathematics
Number of Participants: 10-30
Time: 30-45 minutes
Activity Level: Moderate-High
Props: 30-50 Foot Rope

Set Up:

Lay the rope across the middle of the room.

Objective:

Solve the riddle to cross through the "portal."

Step by Step:

1. Assemble the group on one side of the rope.
2. Explain that the goal of the team is to get across to the other side of the rope by using the formula 1+2+3= (number of participants in the group).
3. Get a volunteer or helper to help you by grabbing one end of the rope.
4. Grab the end opposite of the rope and both you and your volunteer start swinging it in a circle like a jump rope.
5. To effectively solve the riddle, one participant must either run through the open space under the rope or jump over the rope once. After that, 2 participants must do the same thing. Finally, 3 people will go through the portal. The code will reset after this, meaning that 1 person will go next (the number of participants passing through should be 1,2,3,1,2,3,1,2,3 etc.).

Step by Step:

6. Continue doing this until someone fails to get through the rope or gets hit by it. If that happens, have everyone start over at the beginning.
7. If the number of participants during the final pass through the portal is not the same as the current round of the riddle (If one participant is left at the end, and the riddle calls for 3 participants, 2 must run around the portal and join the last participant in crossing).
8. The goal is accomplished when every participant is on the opposite side of the room than they started.

Questions for Discussion:

- How would you describe the riddle?

- What were some of the ideas that you tried in order to solve the riddle?

Facilitator Notes:

This can be one of the most difficult activities in this book as far as executing a plan. It is difficult to win this activity. Encourage participants to keep trying if they get frustrated, and even go a little slack on the rules if the team has taken a long time completing the objective.

It helps if you are working with another non-participant when swinging the rope. Feel free to give the group planning periods during the activity so that you can rest your arm.The activity usually works best when the facilitator is as ambiguous as possible with the riddle. Answer questions vaguely if at all.

Magnetic Human Chain

Magnets can be found in many applications across the STEM fields. This activity is a fun way to teach participants about polarity of magnets.

STEM Field: Science
Number of Participants: 10-100
Time: 10-20 minutes
Activity Level: Moderate
Props: None

Set Up:

None.

Objective:

Try to avoid becoming a bigger magnet.

Step by Step:

1. Have everyone spread out across the activity area and ask the participants get into pairs.
2. In the pairs, each participant can choose one of two polarities: positive or negative. To choose positive, participants will cross their arms in front of them like a plus sign. Negative is a horizontal arm in front of the body like a minus sign.
3. Have each pair turn back to back. On the count of 3, they will turn around and show their sign.
4. If the participants choose the same sign, they maybe go and find another person to play against.
5. If the participants choose opposite signs, the polarities attract, and the participants must link arms or hold hands.

Step by Step:

6. The new magnet made of two participants must go find another magnet made of two participants to play against. This time, each magnet must decide together which polarity to choose.
7. If the participants choose the same sign, they find another magnet made of two participants. If they choose opposite signs, they become a four person magnet.
8. Magnets may only play against other magnets of the same size.
9. Magnets will continue to grow and link together until there is a very large magnet, a few middle magnets, and a small magnet. The small magnet is the winner!

Questions for Discussion:

- Which parts of magnets attract?
- Why was it hard for large groups to keep from growing?
- How did the small magnet win?

Facilitator Notes:

Make sure everyone engages. Encourage participants to just play and have fun with it!

Maze Run

In technology, communication can either make or break a program or device. Without specific instruction written in the code, problems can arise in operation. This activity shows the importance of specificity.

STEM Field: Technology
Number of Participants: 9-30
Time: 25-40minutes
Activity Level: Moderate
Props: Blindfolds, ropes or tape, optional obstacles (pillows, stuffed animals, chairs, etc.)

Set Up:

Create a 20' x 20' maze on the ground using the tape and ropes. Place obstacles in the path of the maze. Split the group up into teams of three.

Objective:

Get the blindfolded participant through the maze as fast as possible.

Step by Step:

1. Have each group nominate one participant to be blindfolded. This person is the program.
2. Have each group nominate one participant to lose verbal communication. This person is the programmer.
3. It is very important that the final person in each group does not look at the maze at all. This person is the compiler.
4. Place the compiler from each group with their backs facing the maze. Instruct them to never turn around or look at the maze.

Step by Step:

5. Place the programmers at the entrance to the maze, it is their job to walk through the maze and memorize the path step by step, thereby "writing the code." To facilitate this, give each programmer a piece of paper and pen/marker.
6. After the programmers have made their way through the maze, have them stand in front of their own compilers. As each team becomes ready, have them place the blindfolded programs in front of the maze.
7. Without speaking, each programmer must give their paper (or code) to his or her own compiler to get the program through the maze.
8. By speaking to the programs, the compilers will guide them through the maze and to the exit. They will not look at the maze. They will read the code given to them by the programmer while their back is still to the maze. It is often a good idea to use the programmers as a safety precaution. They can help the blindfolded participants be safe in the maze.
9. When each team is done, allow them to turn around and take the blindfolds off.

Questions for Discussion:

- What one word would you use to describe this activity?

- What made this activity difficult?

Maze Run

Questions for Discussion:

- Why do programmers need to be specific when coding?

Facilitator Notes:

*****It is very important to ensure and instill a sense of trust within the group before attempting this activity. Please do not try Maze Run before building trust on a smaller/safer level.

Safety is primary! Make sure that the group is ready and comfortable enough for blindfolds. Always ask the blindfolded participants if they are ok being blindfolded.

Make sure that the blindfolded participants do not run into any obstructions. This is why pillows are sometimes used to line the edge of the maze.

If groups are having a particularly hard time with this activity, remind them to be as specific as possible. This often helps

Meteor Shower

In almost every aspiring astronomer's life, there was a night that he or she went outside after midnight to look up at the sky and marvel at a beautiful meteor shower. This activity is a fun way to recreate a meteor shower while getting to know each other a little better.

STEM Field: Science
Number of Participants: 20-70
Time: 10-20 minutes
Activity Level: Medium
Props: Colorful paper, markers

Set Up:

Give each participant a piece of paper and a marker.

Objective:

Don't get hit by the meteorites!

Step by Step:

1. Explain to the participants that meteoroids are small pieces of rock and debris that float around in space. Each one of these have special properties.
2. Just like the meteoroids, the participants all have something that makes them unique. Have everyone write 3 interesting facts about themselves on their own pieces of paper.
3. Now that everyone has their own meteoroids, have them crumple the pieces of paper into compact balls. The meteoroids are hitting Earth's atmosphere and becoming more dense, transforming the meteoroids into meteors.

Meteor Shower

Step by Step:

4. Once the meteors are crumpled into balls, have everyone make a meteor shower by throwing the meteors into the air.
5. As the meteors hit the "Earth's surface" they become meteorites! Everyone should try to avoid being hit by the meteorites at all cost!
6. Now that the meteorites have hit the surface, an all-out meteorite war breaks loose. Holding no more than 1 "meteorite" at a time, participants will try to hit other participants with the paper balls while avoiding being hit.
7. After 2-3 minutes of the meteorite war, have each participant grab 1 meteorite each and try to find the original owner by looking at the interesting facts on the inside.
8. The activity ends once everyone has found his or her own meteorite.

Questions for Discussion:

- What is the difference between a meteoroid, meteor, and meteorite?

- Who was hit the least by meteorites?

Facilitator's Notes:

Safety is most important. Make sure that no participants will hit others in the face with the paper balls.

If a participant has a hard time coming up with 3 interesting facts about his or herself, encourage them to write where they are from, who they look up to, and his or her favorite food.

Paper Airplane Contest

Participants learn aerodynamics through trial and error.

STEM Field: Science
Number of Participants: 5-50
Time: 20-40 minutes
Activity Level: Low
Props: Colorful Paper (paperclips are optional)

Set Up:

Have all of the participants stand in a single rank line.

Objective:

Craft and throw a projectile as far as possible. The airplane that goes the longest distance is the winner.

Step by Step:

1. Start the activity by giving the participants 3-5 minutes to craft paper projectiles (usually airplanes).
2. On the count of three, have the group throw their airplanes as far from the line as they can. Declare a winner for the first round.
3. Have each participant retrieve their projectile and cross back over the line to his or her starting position.
4. Give the group another planning period to revise their projectile designs.
5. Repeat steps 2-4.
6. Give the group one final attempt to throw their projectiles. This time, everyone should be a lot farther than they were originally. Declare the final winner.

Questions for Discussion:

- How could you have made the planes go farther?
- What were some different designs that you used?
- Could you have done better with another try?

Facilitator Notes:

It usually encourages the group bond if you allow participants to help each other. We are all trying to help each other grow!

Variations:

1. Have the participants draw a goal that he or she has in their life on the paper. Now, as the plane goes farther and farther each round, the participant will unknowingly connect that feeling to his or her goal. This is a great way to teach persistence and determination in goal setting and achieving. Allowing others to help craft airplanes in this round shows that the group is also supportive of each other's dreams.

Play Doh Debrief

A major portion of STEM involves creativity. Participants have a chance to express themselves freely with this simple debrief. It also encourages the more ordered and analytical participants to create structure..

STEM Field: Engineering
Number of Participants: 5-20
Time: 5-10 minutes
Activity Level: Low
Pool Party: Break the Ice
Props: A small tub of Play-Doh for each participant, or large tubs to share.

Set Up:

Give each participant his or her favorite color of Play Doh and sit in a circle.

Objective:

Create.

Step by Step:

1. As soon as the participants receive the Play Doh, they will want to begin molding and shaping it into something. This is perfect.
2. Ask the participants to create a sculpture out of the Play Doh that represents how they felt during the previous activity.
3. Have everyone in the circle share what they sculpted and why.

Facilitator Notes:

Disallow any destructive attitudes or actions toward other participants' sculptures.

Popcorn

In engineering, the ability to work together while maintaining individual tasks is imperative. Popcorn will get your participants moving as they learn to work together to achieve a common goal and learn the design process.

STEM Field: Engineering
Number of Participants: 5-20
Time: 20-30 minutes
Activity Level: Moderate
Props: Popcorn Kit or a mop bucket, small rope (15-20'), enough large Wiffle and small Wiffle balls to fill the bucket.

Set Up:

Place a bucket in the middle of an open area on the floor. Place a rope circle around the bucket that is about 5-7 feet in diameter. The bucket will be almost overflowing with Wiffle balls.

Objective:

As a group, participants will bounce the Wiffle balls inside the rope circle and into the bucket as quickly as possible during four rounds.

Step by Step:

1. There will be four 1-minute rounds.
2. The participants cannot stand inside the rope circle.
3. The participants must bounce the Wiffle balls inside the rope circle into the bucket. No tossing the Wiffle balls directly into the bucket.
4. The goal is to get all of the Wiffle balls into the bucket within the 1-minute rounds.

Step by Step:

5. The participants must have their back turned to the bucket while the facilitator empties the contents onto the floor.
6. If a participant is holding a Wiffle ball, they can not move their feet. They are stuck in that position until they get rid of the ball.
7. When each round is over and the facilitator stops the timer the group must stop throwing the Wiffle balls.

Questions for Discussion:

- What word best describes round 1?
- What word best describes round 4?
- What actions or plans did you implement to become more efficient and productive?
- What could have been done to improve the team's performance?
- If you were teaching a new team how to complete this activity, what things would you tell the team?
- How did you redesign your system to achieve effectiveness?

Facilitator Notes:

The best way for the team to complete this activity is if the participants lay around the bucket, creating a barrier that keeps the balls from scattering across the room.

Popcorn

Facilitator Notes:
A great debrief for this activity involves the process of design and redesign. During the first round, participants had to learn to work with the materials they were given.

After that, each round became increasingly better through the use of planning and redesigning the system used by the group.

This activity only works if done on a hard surface. This does not really work effectively on grass or extremely soft carpet.

Variation:
1. For very large groups you can use more than one Popcorn kit, and Wiffle balls could go to either bucket. All the other rules apply for the larger groups.

Probability Cards

Probability and statistic play a big part in many fields of mathematics. This activity is a fun way to teach probability and teamwork.

STEM Field: Mathematics
Number of Participants: 5-52
Time: 15-25 minutes
Activity Level: Low
Props: A deck of playing cards.

Set Up:

None.

Objective:

Get as far as possible in the deck by guessing which card will not appear next.

Step by Step:

1. Have the group form a single file line facing you.
2. Shuffle the deck in front of the participants to show that the activity is fair.
3. One at a time, the participants will walk to the front of the line and tell you which card will not be next (king, ace, 7, etc.). If they are correct, and the card they said is different than the card shown, the next person moves up and the round continues.
4. If the card that you flip over is the same as the participant said, reshuffle the deck and begin again.
5. After each round, ask the group to set a goal. Maybe they can even get through a whole deck.

Probability Cards

Questions for Discussion:

- What were some ways to help you know which card will not be next?
- Was there ever a point when you new for certain what the next card was?
- Why did you guess the card you guessed?
- Did you think this activity was impossible?
- Did you get frustrated at any point during the activity?

Facilitator Notes:

Allow the participants to talk to each other and reason out the probabilities. If the group completes the activity quickly, take this ability away.

Put It Together

Participants gain a better understanding of technology by seeing how everything fits together.

STEM Field: Technology
Number of Participants: 2-20
Time: 10-30 minutes
Activity Level: Low
Props: A disassembled television remote or computer keyboard, a screwdriver, markers, colorful paper.

Set Up:

Place the pieces of the disassembled device on a table (make sure to keep the screws or bolts visible).

Objective:

To assemble the device as quickly as possible.

Step by Step:

1. Take about 1 minutes to allow the participants to view all of the pieces of the disassembled device.
2. Give the participants a 3-5 minute planning period on how to best assemble the device. Encourage them to use drawings or blueprints to show ideas. Make sure that no participants look at the device parts.
3. Begin the timer and have the participants reassemble the device. Stop the timer when there are no parts left, and you have the device in whole.

Questions for Discussion:

- What was the easiest part of that activity? Hardest?

Put It Together

Questions for Discussion:

- How did the planning period help you reassemble the device?
- How did having multiple people in the group help you accomplish the goal?

Facilitator Notes:

While this activity largely focused on how devices are assembled, it also provides a good chance for the participants to work as a team and create a strategy for multiple people to execute.

Encourage the group with a time bonus if everyone in the group contributes to the reassembly. This will help the more active participants engage the less active participants.

Variations:

1. To make the activity more difficult, take away the participants' verbal communication. It becomes a lot harder if no one can speak.If the group is particularly strong as a group, blindfold some of the more knowledgable or active members of the group. ***** It is imperative that the group is ready to use blindfolds. Many participants can become anxious if they have not grown to trust the group. Always make sure to ask participants if they are comfortable wearing a blindfold before the activity.

Puzzle Cubes

Participants challenge each others' design and special skills by designing and manufacturing real puzzle cubes.

STEM Field: Engineering
Number of Participants: 3-30
Time: 20-40 minutes
Activity Level: Low
Props: 27 small wooden blocks or dice per person/team, super glue (or carpenter's glue if you have enough time for it to dry), paper, pencils or pens.

Set Up:

Lay out 27 blocks, a piece of paper, and a writing utensil for each participant/team.

Objective:

Design and create a 3x3x3 puzzle cube, then challenge each other to solve the cubes you made.

Step by Step:

1. Explain that an imaginary wood; (or plastic for the dice) manufacturing plant has designed a new process that leaves small blocks of wood (or plastic) as by-products of the manufacturing.
2. It is now each participant's job as the factory engineer to design a puzzle cube that makes profit from the otherwise useless blocks.
3. The participants create pieces for these 3x3x3 puzzle cubes by gluing the individual pieces together.

Step by Step:

4. There are constraints that each puzzle must abide by so that the "consumer" finds the cubes challenging:
   A. Each puzzle piece may be no less than 3 and no more than 6 blocks.
   B. Each puzzle must contain 5 and only 5 pieces.
   C. Each puzzle piece must be 3 dimensional, meaning that the cubes extend in length, width, and depth.
   D. Participants must design each piece on paper before creating the puzzle.
5. After the participants have designed their puzzles, have them create the puzzle pieces by glueing the blocks/dice together as designed.
6. After the glue dries, have the participants challenge each other to see who's puzzle was the best!

Questions for Discussion:

- Why might an engineer decide to build a puzzle cube?

- What other ways can an engineer come up with designs that save or make money?

- Why was it important that you designed each piece before creating it?

Facilitator Notes:

Each constraint that was added makes the cube more challenging, but it can also take up a little more time in the activity. Feel free to add constraints to make the activity more challenging, or take away constraints to make the activity a little faster.

Ringer

The laws of physics and thermodynamics can sometimes overwhelm students. This activity is a ton of fun, and gives students first hand examples of these laws. Especially, Newton's Three Laws of Motion.

STEM Field: Science
Number of Participants: 2-30
Time: 20 minutes plus
Activity level: Medium
Props: Rope, 20 balls in a variety of size, weight, and kind.

Set Up:

Group participants into 2 or more teams.

Objective:

Like classic games of "marbles," teams try to knock balls out of the circle with their "shooter" ball, thereby scoring points. This demonstration teaches laws of momentum and weight transfer.

Step By Step:

1. Refresh the students about Newton's Three Laws of Motion:
   A. Every object in a state of uniform motion tends to remain in that state of motion unless an external force is applied to it.
   B. The relationship between an object's mass m, its acceleration a, and the applied force F is F = ma. Acceleration and force are vectors (as indicated by their symbols being displayed in slant bold font); in this law the direction of the

Step By Step:

force vector is the same as the direction of the acceleration vector.

C. For every action there is an equal and opposite reaction.

1. Make a circle on the ground with your rope. The circle can be as big as you'd like -- generally speaking, 10 feet across. Note: The bigger the circle, the harder it is to win! Be sure to use a flat surface.
2. Set up the balls in the middle. You can do this however you like. A plus sign is fairly standard, but you can also make a circle or just scatter them randomly. Use anywhere from 5 - 15 balls.
3. Have the first team throw their ball (called the shooter). They can sit or stand anywhere outside of the circle on the first go. The aim is to hit another ball out of the circle while keeping the shooter in. They must throw underhanded and roll the ball (sort of like bowling).
4. If the team successfully knocked out another ball (while keeping their shooter in), have them go again. They receive a point. When they go again, they must throw from where the shooter landed.
5. If the first team didn't knock out a marble, the second team gets their turn. If they knock out the other player's shooter, they don't get a point or to keep the shooter, but the other player does have to shoot from outside the circle (which is much more difficult) on their next turn. It's sort of like an automatic "lose your turn" move.
6. Finish the game when all the balls are gone. Whichever team knocked out the most balls wins.

Questions for Discussion:

- How did you see Newton's 1st law of motion in action?
- How did you see Newton's 1st law of motion in action?
- How did you see Newton's 1st law of motion in action?
- What is the difference in an elastic and an inelastic collision?

Facilitator Notes:

This activity can seem to have many steps, however, it is important to remind the students that the game is a simple and fun way to describe physics.

.

Robots

Participants learn how to control and become robots.

STEM Field: Technology
Number of Participants: 10-72
Time: 10-20 minutes
Activity Level: Medium-High
Props: None

Set Up:

Make sure the participants are in a large enough area to walk/run around.

Objective:

Have fun and become robots!

Step by Step:

1. Have each participant get into a pair. Once the participant is paired up, have one participant from each team volunteer to be a controller and the other participant volunteers and the robot.
2. Once each controller/robot team has been decided, explain that the controller has a few commands that can be given to the robot.
3. Rules for Controllers:
   A. A single tap on the middle of the back means "Go."
   B. Two taps on the middle of the back means "Stop."
   C. A tap on the left shoulder means a ninety degree turn to the left.
   D. A tap on the right shoulder means a ninety degree turn to the right.

Step by Step:

4. Now it is time for the robots' instructions:
   A. At the beginning of each round, the robots will power down. The controllers have to find a way to power them on.
   B. Robots follow all controls of the controller.
   C. Robots can move at whichever speed they want.
   D. If a robot is about to move away from the activity area or run into another robot, the safety mechanism goes into place.
5. Have each participant practice the safety mechanism gesture. One that works well for us is having each student throw up their arms, wave them side to side in small arcs, and say "System Overload" repeatedly.
6. Once the first round is over, have the controllers and robots switch places.
7. After the second round, have each group pair up with another group. Feel free to join a group if there is one that doesn't have four participants in it.
8. Have each group nominate one person as a robot and three people as controllers. Each robot now takes commands from all three controllers.
9. After this round, have each robot switch places with his or her controllers. This round is hilarious to watch!

Questions for Discussion:

- What was the best part of being a controller/robot?

- What was the hardest part about being a controller/robot?

Questions for Discussion:

- How did different robots act different even though they had the same design?
- In what ways did the different robot designs make the activity challenging?

Facilitator Notes:

The best part of this game is how much fun the participants have. While the debrief and lesson is centered around the idea that technologies with the same design can have different functions or quality, it is imperative that this activity encourages participants to have fun and play.

Safety is always a first priority for these activities, so make sure that the participants are not running each other over or leaving the activity area.

Rube Goldberg

This activity is a fun and challenging rest of engineering skills. It places emphasis on the iterative engineering design process, communication, teamwork, creativity, and working with limited resources.

STEM Field: Engineering
Number of Participants: 8-40
Time: 60-90 minutes
Activity Level: Moderate
Props: Jenga blocks (a lot cheaper than dominoes), string, tape, rope, a bucket for each team, 6 tennis balls, books, chairs, anything that could be used for a rube-Goldberg machine.

Set Up:

Split the group into 2-3 teams. Give an equal amount of varied objects to each team. Place tape boundaries between each team.

Objective:

Create the longest, most creative Rube-Goldberg machine possible (think of the machine at the beginning of *Back to the Future*).

Step by Step:

1. After giving each team the materials and placing them inside their boundaries, give the participants 30 minutes-1 hour to create the most creative machine with as many segments as possible.

2. Score is based on:
   A. Longest segment.
   B. Most segments.
   C. Longest Rube-Goldberg Machine.
   D. Most creative segment.
   E. Coolest end result.
3. If the group has a hard time coming up with final results for the Rube-Goldberg machine, have them try to roll the tennis ball into the bucket.
4. After the allotted time, judge the machines and declare a winner!

Questions for Discussion:

- Why did you use that specific design?

- How many times did it take to finally get the desired result?

- How does the design process repeat?

Facilitator Notes:

Usually, we like to give the teams space to design and build the machines on their own. If a team has a question for you about design or how something works, feel free to give suggestions or examples, but don't tell them how to build the machine.

Sensors

In living things, there are sensors that allow us to feel pain, be gentle easily, and detect when we've felt something. This activity shows a machine's point of view.

STEM Field: Technology
Number of Participants: 2-30
Time: 5-10 minutes
Activity Level: Low
Props: A pair of thick work gloves or gardening gloves for every two participants.

Set Up:

Have the group split up into teams of 2. Each team needs at least 1 person with shoestrings on their shoes. Have each participant wear one of the work gloves.

Objective:

As a team, tie the shoe.

Step by Step:

1. For the first round, allow the participants to work together tying the shoe using each of their ungloved hands.
2. After each team has successfully tied the shoe of one of its participants, have the team try the same activity while using the gloved hands of each person.

Questions for Discussion:

- Why was that so hard?

- How does this relate to technology?

Seven

Participants try to count as high as possible with numbers that are associated with seven.

STEM Field: Mathematics
Number of Participants: 5-50
Time: 5-20 minutes
Activity Level: Low
Props: None

Set Up:

Assemble the group into a circle.

Objective:

Count as high as possible without saying any number that contains seven or is divisible by seven.

Step by Step:

1. After explaining the objective to the group, give them a practice round. One volunteer or nominee will start by saying "1." The person to his or her right or left will say "2." This continues around the circle.
2. When someone gets to the number seven, they should make a buzzer sound rather than saying "7."
3. The group will continue counting while they avoid numbers that are divisible by seven (e.g. 14) and numbers that contain seven (e.g. 17).
4. If a participant takes too long to come up with the appropriate number or sound, or if someone says the incorrect number or sound, the whole group will raise their arms, yell "Ooooooooohhhhh well," and then drop their arms in the "Oh well" gesture.

Step by Step:
5. This game can continue for as long as you'd like!

Questions for Discussion:

- Was this harder than you imagined at first?

- Did your group fall into a pattern?

- What ways could we make this activity easier?

- What ways could we make this activity more challenging?

Facilitator Notes:
If the participants start to fall into a pattern of saying the same number over and over, feel free to mix things up by choosing a different person to start the count.

A great way to frame this activity is to have the group set a goal for themselves. After that goal is reached, have them set a new goal. See if they can make it past the 70's!

Variations:
1. If you are working with a particularly adept group, "3" is a much harder activity. 3 is the exact same game, except no numbers with 3 in them or divisible by 3 may be called.

Simple Machines

In the field of machinery and robotics, it is not one machine that completes a task, rather a combination of various machines with different capabilities, strengths, and weaknesses. This activity shows how a robot uses the power of synergy to achieve a goal.

STEM Field: Technology
Number of Participants: 10-25
Time: 30-40 minutes
Activity Level: Moderate
Props: Two ropes or tape to mark boundary lines, a beach ball, and a large room.

Set Up:

Place the boundary lines on opposite sides of the room about 5-10 feet from each wall. Have the participants gather between on of the walls and the boundary line on that side. Place the beach ball on the ground in front of them, just on the other side of the line.

Objective:

Move the ball from one side of the room to the other as efficiently as possible.

Step by Step:

1. Explain to the group that no one may carry the beach ball. Instead, each participant will act as a machine to accomplish a certain task.
2. The 4 machine types are:
   A. The Lifters: These participants are allowed to lift the beach ball off the ground. Lifters may not move their feet, throw the ball, or rotate

Step by Step:

their bodies. They are allowed to extend their arms and bend over.

B. The Rotators: Rotators are used to grab the ball once it is in the air and rotate it around in any of 360 degrees. Rotators may not move their feet, throw the ball, or bend down to get the ball off the ground. They are allowed to extend their arms and rotate the ball toward any direction.

C. The Pushers: Pushers are used to move robots that are not currently in use. Pushers may not bend down, touch the ball, or rotate. They are allowed to push on the backs of other machines to move them. After a pusher performs their action twice, they are no longer allowed to push. At that point they can be used to hold the ball only. Pushers may extend their arms.

D. The Walkers: Walkers are used to carry the ball a short distance. Walkers may not bend down or move other robots. They are allowed to carry the ball while walking. Walkers may only walk in a square made of two paces per side.

3. The participants must decide as a group on which machines will be used to cross the playing field.
4. The number of each type of machine may not exceed 1/3 of the group's size (If there are 21 participants, there can be no more than 7 of each type).
5. When the beach ball crossed the line on the opposite side of the room, the group has completed the goal.

Questions for Discussion:

- What was difficult about that activity?
- Why can't one machine complete the activity alone?
- Which machine was the most important? (None of them!)

Facilitator Notes:

f the group is convinced that they can't get the beach ball across the line with their current design, allow them to restart and redesign of they wish.

If the group accomplishes the activity too easily, have them take the beach ball to the opposite side and back to win. This is a good idea if you are working in a smaller space.

Walkers may only walk in one direction for two steps, but it doesn't matter how big those steps are (don't tell them that, though!)

STEM Joboo

For young participants, STEM careers are often grouped into a few big-name jobs like doctor or biologist. This activity helps participants expand their lines of site to learn about many different kinds of STEM careers.

STEM Field: Science
Number of Participants: 4-50
Time: 5-15 minutes
Activity Level: Low
Props: Joboo Cards. You can copy the Joboo Cards below but also download a printable PDF at www.myparadigmshift.org/stemdownloads.

Set Up:

Split the group up into two equally sized teams and have them form a circle. Give each participant a card, but make sure he or she does not look at it.

Objective:

Race against the other team to figure out which jobs are being described.

Step by Step:

1. Have each team nominate a participant to go first.
2. When the facilitator says "Go," have the first participant flip his or her card over.
3. The participant must describe the career listed on the card without using any of the words on the card.
4. If the participant says one of the words on the card, have them grab a new card and go to the end of the circle.

STEM Joboo

Step by Step:

5. After the group correctly guessed the first career, the second participant will take his or her turn.
6. The first team to correctly guess all of the careers wins!

Questions for Discussion:

- What was one of the most interesting careers that you heard?

- How important is it to go to a college that offers the major that you want?

Facilitator Notes:

This activity pretty much plays itself. Just make sure the participants aren't cheating.

Oncologist	Engineer	Teacher
Cancer Doctor Chemotherapy Radiation Hair	Create Fix Machine Build Bridges	Teach Student School Homework Class
Nurse	**Archaeologist**	**Astronaut**
Hospital Doctor Patient Help Medicine	Bones Dinosaur Dig Old Dirt	Space Moon Rocket Shuttle Helmet

Technology Line-Up

Participants choose which technological advance has been the most important/beneficial.

STEM Field: Technology
Number of Participants: 3-25
Time: 15-30 minutes
Activity Level: Low
Props: Markers and colorful paper.

Set Up:

Give each participant a marker and three pieces of paper. Have the participants sit in a circle or group.

Objective:

Come up with some of the greatest technological advances of all time and then rank them as a group. By the end, the group will have decided on a definitive top 10.

Step by Step:

1. Ask the participants to brainstorm technology out loud.
2. If the group agrees that the technology given was a good answer, have the person write down their answer on one of their pieces of paper.
3. This goes until the group has about 10-20 technological advances that have changed the world.
4. As a group, the participants now have to rank the technologies that were proposed (there should be one list for the entire group).

5. By placing the papers on the ground/table and ranking them in order, the group will come up with the 10 greatest inventions of all time.

Questions for Discussion:

- Why did we place more value in certain technologies over others?
- How did the group qualify "better" technologies?
- Did anyone use different criteria for ranking than anyone else?

Facilitator Notes:

It is easy to spend a lot of time arguing minor details, so if a debate lasts for a long time and participants start to get bored or stuck, it's a good idea to "bubble up" the ideas.

This means that you compare the current idea with the one on the bottom of the list. If the idea is better, it is put up against the second idea from the bottom. This way, a place is found for the idea quickly and effectively.

Don't forget to remind participants that not all technologies are electrical. Can you imagine a world without the knife, fire, or plumbing?

Variations:

1. A fun way to get the participants to learn more about each other is to have them share their opinion on which technology is best when they introduce themselves to the other participants.

Tower of Hanoi

One of the most important skills in dealing with mathematics is mathematical reasoning. In this activity, participants will complete The Tower of Hanoi to practice reasoning and mathematical logic.

STEM Field: Mathematics
Number of Participants: 5-30
Time: 10-30 minutes
Activity Level: Low
Props: Colorful paper, scissors, tape/rope

Set Up:

Cut out circles from the paper with diameters of 2, 3, 4, 5, 6, and 7 inches. You should have six paper circles of different colors and diameters. Place three blank pieces of paper on the ground as placeholders. Place the rope/tape line on the ground and assemble the group on the side opposite from the puzzle

Objective:

One piece at a time, move the tower from the placeholder on the left to the placeholder on the right.

Step by Step:

1. For the first round, place the 2," 4," and 6" circles on the left placeholder paper starting with the largest circle on bottom and the smallest circle on top.
2. One at a time, the participants will cross over the tape/rope and move one of the circles to a different placeholder, then cross back to the starting side. Only that participant may be across the line; never more than one at a time.

Step by Step:

3. Participants may not place a larger circle on top of a smaller circle. (The 2" can not be under the 6").
4. The participant may choose to place a circle on either of the two placeholders as long as the move complies with Step #3.
5. Once each participant has used their turn, they may not cross the line again until every other participant has gone.
6. The round is over when the group has assembled the same tower seen at the beginning of the activity, except on the placeholder to the right. The perfect score for this round is seven moves.
7. For the next round, add another circle. Keep only three placeholders. The round plays exactly the same as before, except the team should begin and end with a tower of four circles places from largest on the bottom to smallest on top. The perfect score for this round is 15 moves.
8. Continue adding circles and making the activity more difficult until you are ready to end the activity. The perfect score for five circles is 31 moves. If the group is adept enough to try it, the perfect score for six circle is 63 moves.

Questions for Discussion:

- What patterns did you notice while completing the puzzle?

- What made the activity hard?

- When did you notice the pattern?

Virus Tag

Participants gain an understanding of how viruses work.

STEM Field: Science
Number of Participants: 10+
Time: 5-20 minutes
Activity Level: High
Props: None

Set Up:

Make sure the participants have plenty of room to run around.

Objective:

The person that is "It" (also known as "The Virus") must infect the other participants (also known as "Cells"). The viruses win by infecting everyone and turning the cells into hosts for the virus.

Step by Step:

1. Ask the group for a volunteer. That person is the virus.
2. Since viruses naturally have few enzymes, the viruses are slower than the cells and must walk. Cells can still run.
3. After a virus tags a cell, the cell takes about three seconds to become a host for the virus. This means that the cell still acts like a cell for about three seconds before acting like a virus.
4. By the end of the activity, there should be a full group of viruses and just a few regular cells. These cells are the winners. If no one is left, the virus wins.

What's the Matter?

Students learn about the states of matter and ideal gas laws by looking from a more personal perspective.

STEM Field: Science
Number of Participants: 8-80
Time: 10-20 minutes
Activity Level: Medium
Props: None

Set Up:

Take the participants to a large space. They should have enough area to walk around rapidly while expanding and contracting the activity area.

Objective:

To simulate the activity of solids, liquids, and gasses by moving about in an area without bumping into another "molecule". Students should learn the concept of ideal gas laws (PV=nRT).

Step by Step:

1. Have the participants find their own space in the activity area. If a participant makes contact with another molecule, they are eliminated.
2. At the beginning of the activity, explain that each of the participants are going to live a day in the life of a molecule.
3. Each "molecule" begins the activity as a solid. In all solids, the molecules are in a fixed position and can not move. The molecules of each solid must "vibrate," as is the case with real world solids. This can be done by swaying, wiggling, or slight shuffling.

Step by Step:

4. After the participants get a feel for being a solid, explain that the activity area is beginning to warm up. This means that the fixed solids are beginning to move around slowly in the activity area. At this point, the solids have now become liquids.
5. Since liquids take the shape of their containers, the students will naturally begin to expand to the borders of the activity area, so as to avoid other molecules and elimination. Feel free to begin to tweak the "variables" of the activity area. This includes the size of the area, the "temperature," and the number of participants.
6. As the activity goes on and participants begin to get eliminated, start to heat up the activity area again. This makes your liquids into gasses. The participants should begin to get faster and faster.
7. If the eliminated participants begin to get bored, increase the number of molecules in the "container" by sending the eliminated participants back into the activity area.
8. You should notice at this point that the participants tend to follow the ideal gas laws, namely that the pressure of the container increases when the temperature increases, the size decreases, or the number or participants increases. It is more difficult for the molecules to avoid each other.
9. After the molecules have had plenty of fun and understand the concepts behind the states of matter, have the group "sublime" from gasses back into solids. This is the perfect point in the activity to reflect on what happened.

Questions for Discussion:

- How did changing the temperature affect the difficulty to avoid each other?

- How did changing the area of the activity affect the difficulty?

- Which was more difficult: when the area got warmer or when more molecules were added to the area?

Facilitator Notes:

It is easy for some students to sabotage other molecules. This is usually done jokingly. Sometimes, the older participants will begin to roughhouse.

This problem can be quickly solved by sharing expectations with the group. Often, participants begin to get bored if separated from the activity for too long. This game is designed to re-introduce these participants after a short time.

Paradigm Shift

Paradigm Shift offers leadership training and development with a primary focus to create opportunities for leaders to lead intentionally.

The Paradigm Shift consultants use practical leadership & adventure-based models to help leaders develop powerful relationships, set SMART goals, create personal responsibility, and develop a defined purpose.

We invite our participants to learn through dynamic keynotes, interactive workshops, online coaching, and customized training. Most importantly, Paradigm Shift will challenge your team to develop into leaders.

Find Paradigm Shift online at :

www.myparadigmshift.org

Leadership Camps

Paradigm Shift will change the way you do camps. An exciting trend for educational and faith-based organizations is hosting a leadership camp for students. These camps incorporate a variety of aspects of your program, and have drastically increased student engagement.

Camps can be 1-5 days and held during summer break, spring break, or even a weekend. Paradigm Shift specializes in designing every aspect of these incredible camps. Each camp will be focused on your program's objectives and desires.

Workshops

Each workshop is custom designed to work with your program's desired goals in mind. All workshops incorporate experiential learning (learning through a reflection of doing) and provide groups of all experience levels opportunities to create and enhance their leadership skills.

Our leadership workshops focus on strengths-based learning to cultivate powerful results. The Paradigm Shift staff creates every workshop based on your current curriculum, props and staff to develop an individualized event perfect your program!

Keynotes

The Paradigm Shift team treats their keynotes as more than a lecture. It is a conversation. It is powerful. It is fun. More than anything, it is an opportunity for the audience to become engaged in the leadership material they are learning and to make it applicable to their own lives.

We use cutting edge theories and techniques from experiential-based learning to infuse leadership into every single one of our keynote addresses. We invite the audience to join us on an adventure of learning in a fresh and challenging way.

Coaching

Would you like individual advice and coaching on how to lead your groups? Paradigm Shift offers individual consulting for trainers who want to take the next step in their facilitation.

Each participant enrolled in the coaching classes will also be involved in an online mastermind group that includes many of the best trainers from around the world. We will look at your programming to fine-tune your skills, update your curriculum, & provide you with individualized opportunities for leadership development.

Train the Trainer

Paradigm Shift specializes in training group leaders who want to make a better connections with their participants. In these specialized trainings, our facilitators will walk you through the steps necessary to create better engagement, promote more powerful relationships, and allow substantial change to occur with a group.

Our curriculum has been proven through years of experience with thousands of groups. We follow the "Pool Party Process," a model that prepares groups to experience incredible learning. These trainings are interactive, engaging and customizable to your program

EmojiCARDS

EmojiCARDS were created for educators, counselors, group leaders, and all individuals who need a creative way to explain emotions to their group.

These cards invite participants to engage in conversation about their emotions, feelings, or experiences. Leaders can use these cards in a multitude of ways – as a processing tool, an icebreaker, leadership initiative, or for just plain fun.

A pack of EmojiCARDS costs $15.

You can order EmojiCARDS for your group on the Paradigm Shift website:

www.myparadigmshift.org/store

EmojiCARDS Guide

The activities in this book take full advantage of the fun, yet powerful emotions that are displayed on EmojiCARDS.

Group leaders of all skill levels and experiences can use EmojiCARDS to promote two separate areas of learning…discovering emotions and processing emotions.

The EmojiCARDS Activity Guide has 20 brand new activities, variations for any group, and lists of 200+ emotions.

The EmojiCARDS Activity Guide costs $15.

You can order the EmojiCARDS Activity Guide for your group on the Paradigm Shift website:

www.myparadigmshift.org/store

Wordles

PARADIGM SHIFT LEADERSHIP WORDLES

Paradigm Shift

Meetings should be fun. Classrooms should be fun. Learning should be fun. Wordles are fun.

Wordles are puzzles that engage participants through experiential learning and critical thinking. Wordles invite those in your group to learn and grow together while searching for the answers on these cards.

Example Wordles:

L   O   A   D = Wide Load
BAN   ANA = Banana Split
GIFIREN = Fire Engine
STA4NCE = For Instance
M1Y L1I1F1E = For Once In My Life

Wordles can be found in the Paradigm Shift online store at www.myparadigmshift.org/store.

Number Puzzles

PARADIGM SHIFT LEADERSHIP NUMBER PUZZLES

Paradigm Shift

Number Equations bring fun STEM ideas into the classroom!

Number Puzzles are puzzles that engage participants through experiential learning and critical thinking. Number Puzzles invite those in your group to learn and grow together while searching for the answers on these cards.

Example Number Puzzles:

0 = Absolute Zero on the Kelvin Scale
2 = Pints in a Quart
3 = Square Root of Nine
12 = Sides of a Dodecagon
24 = Letters in the Greek Alphabet

Number Puzzles can be found in the Paradigm Shift online store at www.myparadigmshift.org/store.

Initialisms

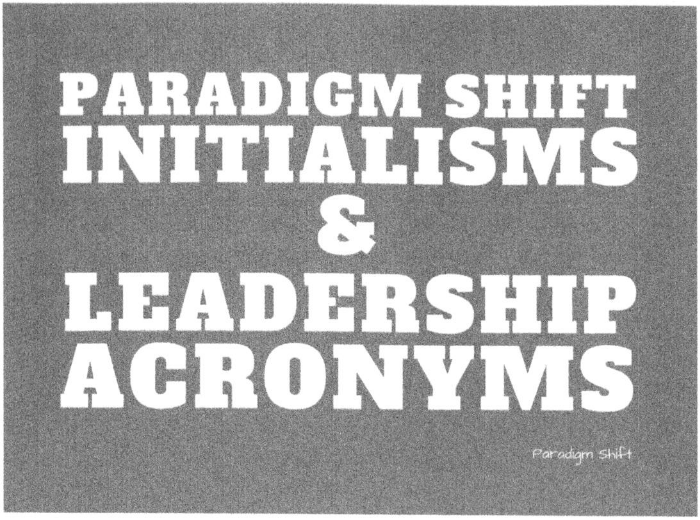

Initialisms challenge the way you view the world and encourage you to learn the history of the acronyms that are all around you!

Initialisms are puzzles that engage participants through experiential learning and critical thinking. Initialisms invite those in your group to learn and grow together while searching for the answers on these cards.

Example Initialisms:

HAZMAT = Hazardous Material
IQ = Intelligence Quotient
NASA = National Aeronautics and Space Administration

Initialisms can be found in the Paradigm Shift online store at www.myparadigmshift.org/store.

Authors

Kyle Price

Kyle has been a part of engineering, robotics, and STEM teams since the eighth grade. As a mentor and team director of design and communication for FIRST robotics team 3152, Kyle has figured out how to effectively lead group conversation and create synergy with STEM teams. Kyle offers keynote addresses to STEM students, teams, and organizations in the areas of goal setting, integrating STEM concepts and theories into holistic leadership, and critical thinking as a member of Paradigm Shift.

Kyle is currently pursuing a degree in Electrical Engineering in the Texas A&M system, and hopes to continue his education to receive his PhD. in Electrical Engineering. He has the privilege to research the exciting field of signal transduction in cellular signaling pathways. He is a member of the National Tutoring Association and the Institute of Electrical and Electronics Engineers, the world's largest professional association for the advancement of technology. When Kyle is not working with STEM groups he can be found watching Premier League football, taking long walks in the park with his calculator, or at a theater near you.

Authors

Ryan Eller

Ryan is the founder and lead consultant of Paradigm Shift, which provides custom-built team-building and leadership training. Ryan has facilitated in 30 US states and hosted leadership conferences in Cuba, Brazil, and Australia. Ryan has the goal of hosting a leadership training in all 50 states and all 7 continents.

Ryan received his Bachelor's Degree in Mass Communication and Master's Degree in Higher Education Administration from Northeastern State University. He is a member of ODSA, SWASAP, and COE. He loves nothing more than a great Nick Collison pick while eating brinner with his beautiful wife Kristin and his little princess Jane.

Jerrod Murr

Murr has been speaking to groups since he was 14. He really stepped up his game in his early twenties. Murr works with small groups in experiential learning settings, as well as keynotes to groups in the thousands. A few speaking highlights include the privilege of planning a leadership conference for over 300 pastors in Cuba, speaking to over 1,000 students in Brazil, and holding the microphone for his kindergarten class song.

Murr currently serves as the Director of 20 Camps and Leadership Develop for Paradigm Shift. He resides in Muskogee, OK with his wife, Jenn, daughter Adelae, and Josalyn. His favorite book is The Giving Tree, and he loves basketball, the OKC Thunder, and good coffee.

Notes

Notes

Notes

Notes

Notes

Printed in Great Britain
by Amazon

61861416R00088